The Professional Teacher
in Further Education

**FURTHER
EDUCATION**

You might also like the following books from Critical Publishing

A Complete Guide to the Level 4 Certificate in Education and Training
By Lynn Machin, Duncan Hindmarch, Sandra Murray and Tina Richardson
978-1-909330-89-4 In print

A Complete Guide to the Level 5 Diploma in Education and Training
By Lynn Machin, Duncan Hindmarch, Sandra Murray and Tina Richardson
978-1-909682-53-5 September 2014

Dial M for Mentor: Critical Reflections on Mentoring for Coaches, Educators and Trainers
By Jonathan Gravells and Susan Wallace
978-1-909330-00-9 In print

Equality and Diversity in Further Education
By Sheine Peart
978-1-909330-97-9 May 2014

Inclusion in Further Education
By Lydia Spenceley
978-1-909682-05-4 June 2014

Teaching and Supporting Adult Learners
By Jackie Scruton and Belinda Ferguson
978-1-909682-13-9 June 2014

The A–Z Guide to Working in Further Education
By Jonathan Gravells and Susan Wallace
978-1-909330-85-6 In print

Understanding the Further Education Sector: A Critical Guide to Policies and Practices
By Susan Wallace
978-1-909330-21-4 In print

Most of our titles are also available in a range of electronic formats. To order please go to our website www.criticalpublishing.com or contact our distributor, NBN International, 10 Thornbury Road, Plymouth PL6 7PP, telephone 01752 202301 or e-mail orders@nbninternational.com.

The Professional Teacher in Further Education

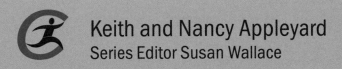

Keith and Nancy Appleyard
Series Editor Susan Wallace

**FURTHER
EDUCATION**

First published in 2014 by Critical Publishing Ltd
Reprinted 2014

British Library Cataloguing in Publication Data
A CIP record for this book is available from the British Library

ISBN: 978-1-909682-01-6

This book is also available in the following e-book formats:

MOBI ISBN: 978-1-909682-02-3
EPUB ISBN: 978-1-909682-03-0
Adobe e-book ISBN: 978-1-909682-04-7

Cover and text design by Greensplash Limited
Project Management by Out of House Publishing
Printed and bound in Great Britain by Bell and Bain Ltd, Glasgow

Critical Publishing
152 Chester Road
Northwich
CW8 4AL
www.criticalpublishing.com

Contents

Acknowledgements

Sincere thanks to:

- Karl Aubrey for his time and expertise;
- Lydia Spenceley and the ITT trainees at Grantham College for their valuable input;
- Greylees Communication Group and Jalon Philosophy Group for their feedback;
- Jools Freeman and Peter Ryan for their helpful comments;
- Julia Morris and Sue Wallace for their advice and ongoing support.

Meet the authors

Keith Appleyard

I have worked in Further Education (FE) since 1978 as a teacher, college senior manager and teacher trainer. Over a 20-year period I was a tutor and course leader for PGCE/Cert Ed programmes at Lincoln College, and a tutor and franchise co-ordinator on these programmes at Nottingham Trent University. Most recently I have worked as an ITT reviewer for Standards Verification UK and as a consultant for LSIS. I live in Lincolnshire and, with my wife Nancy, am the co-author of two books on FE: *The Minimum Core of Language and Literacy* and *Communicating with Learners*.

Nancy Appleyard

My early working life was in the insurance industry, initially with a large general insurance company and then as a partner in a commercial insurance brokerage. A career change brought me to Lincoln College where I taught Business Skills and Communication Studies at Lincoln College for ten years. Since 2001 I have worked as a specialist designing and delivering communication and personal development programmes throughout the wider FE sector in the East Midlands. Along with my husband Keith I enjoy travelling and when home commitments allow us to get away, I do my best to see as much of the world as possible by giving talks to cruise ship audiences.

Meet the series editor

Susan Wallace

I am Emeritus Professor of Education at Nottingham Trent University where, for many years, part of my role was to support learning on the initial training courses for teachers in the Further Education (FE) sector. I taught in the sector myself for ten years, including on BTEC programmes and Basic Skills provision. My particular interest is in the motivation and behaviour of students in FE, and in mentoring and the ways in which a successful mentoring relationship can support personal and professional development. I have written a range of books, mainly aimed at teachers and student teachers in the sector; and I enjoy hearing readers' own stories of FE, whether it's by e-mail or at speaking engagements and conferences.

1 Introduction: the oldest profession

Introduction

An ancient parable from the Indian subcontinent tells the story of the blind men and an elephant.

> One day an elephant was brought to a village where a number of blind men lived. Each of the blind men touched the elephant to find out what an elephant was like. One touched its leg and said an elephant was like a pillar. Another touched its tail and said that an elephant was like a length of rope. Yet another touched its trunk and said that an elephant was like the branch of a tree.

If you were to ask a dozen people what their understanding of professionalism was you may well find that, just like the blind men, they give many different answers. This is because each one's perspective would be based on the professional elephant they were familiar with; a professional football player would have a different concept of professionalism to that of a lawyer or an engineer or a teacher. Even within the teaching profession there isn't necessarily a shared understanding of what professionalism is.

Professionalism may be a slippery term with differing meanings for different people; it is nevertheless an important concept for Further Education (FE) teachers, no matter what stage of their career they have reached. Anyone working in the sector soon comes across the concepts of being a professional, having professional values and identity and so on. Indeed, the vast majority of FE teachers see themselves as professionals and take pride in this status. One of the most severe criticisms that can be made of an FE teacher is that they are in some way unprofessional or that they do not behave in a professional manner; so professional standards are an important feature of a teacher's life in FE.

Much the same problem of definition that surrounds the word 'professionalism' arises when considering what exactly is meant by the term 'Further Education': it means different things to different people. FE is a vast sector that is difficult to be specific about because of its diversity. It is not just a collection of FE colleges but a conglomeration that includes private training providers, local authorities offering adult community learning, industrial training departments of major employers, some National Health Service (NHS) trusts, and training departments of government agencies such as the Ministry of Defence (MoD) and the Prison Service. If you are working within this conglomeration you may be involved in adult or community education, in family or youth work or in commercial training, or you may be working for a charity or voluntary organisation. You could be a full-time teacher with many years' experience or a teacher trainer. Clearly, your concept of what FE is will depend to some extent on which segment of the FE elephant you are familiar with and on your particular teaching role.

Professionalism in the FE sector

Professionalism is not merely an academic concept: FE teachers are operating in a political, social and economic environment that drastically affects their professional practice. One key feature of the political pressures on the FE sector has been successive governments' belief that a high-quality FE system depends on a professional workforce – a body of trained, highly skilled and well-motivated teachers delivering programmes aimed at producing a national workforce capable of engendering economic prosperity.

This has led to government policies of professionalising the role of FE teachers by regulation, exemplified by the introduction in 2007 of a set of mandatory professional standards (LLUK, 2007) that all FE teacher training courses need to meet and which form the basis of a licence to practise that all FE teachers need to hold. In the standards, the word 'professional' occurs dozens of times. Indeed, the first of the five domains that make up the standards is entirely devoted to professional values and practice. Consequently, FE teacher training courses put considerable stress on professional values, professional knowledge and professional practice.

This top-down approach to establishing a professional FE teaching service is currently being modified, with official acceptance that over-prescriptive regulation may reduce professionalism rather than encourage it. Hence the mandatory aspects of the 2007 regulations have been revoked and replaced by a more voluntary approach. This has been accompanied by the formation of a new professional body for FE teachers, the Education and Training Foundation, with the intention that FE teachers and other stakeholders in the sector will have greater influence on the shape of FE in the future.

However, at the time of writing the 2007 professional standards still exist and do provide a framework for an FE teacher's professional values, knowledge, understanding and skills. These standards make a good starting point to examine the nature of professionalism in FE and training.

About this book

This book is essentially an examination of professionalism for teachers working in FE. It explores what it actually means to be a professional FE teacher and how professional excellence can be best achieved. Consequently it is not primarily a 'how to teach' book. Rather the emphasis is on how to achieve excellence through critical analysis of practical teaching situations and the theory underpinning this practice. It is intended to be relevant to your work as an FE teacher, no matter which part of the sector you are working in and what stage of your career you have reached.

Content

The content of the book is designed as a guide for you to improve your professional practice. Theory is introduced to support this aim. The idea is for you to reflect critically about your own professionalism and to use your own experience as well as relevant theory to improve your teaching.

Chapter 2 examines the changing nature of professionalism and how teaching fits into the various interpretations of the term. It considers the influence of government policy on professionalism in FE and suggests a range of qualities that are the basis for your professional values. These qualities are examined in detail in the subsequent two chapters. Chapter 3 concentrates on your self-awareness and professional identity. It considers how your values, beliefs and emotions inform both your teaching and professional relationships. Chapter 4 concerns your professional curiosity about your learners and asks you to examine your own assumptions and judgements. It suggests that professional curiosity better equips you to value and promote diversity.

Chapter 5 is about teacher professionalism in action, illustrating how the main features of professionalism are evident in practical teaching. The chapter's main theme is that critical reflection is the key to developing your professional teaching skills. Chapter 6 focuses on building professional relationships with your learners and offers some features of a 'best' learning experience. Chapter 7 is also about professionalism in action, within your wider role as a member of an academic community. Moving from a review of the management theory of how people function in organisations, the chapter seeks to identify and analyse the professional skills needed to work effectively with colleagues and others.

Chapter 8 considers the professional as a perennial learner and how this relates to your own continuing professional development (CPD). The final chapter summarises the key features of professionalism and suggests ways in which you can enrich your professional life within the context of contemporary FE.

Structure and use

Each chapter, apart from this introduction and the conclusion, follows the same structure that includes:

*   a statement of chapter objectives outlining the purpose and rationale for the chapter, plus a visual map that depicts the chapter content;

*   an introduction briefly outlining the chapter content;

*   case studies giving practical examples of the learning points under consideration, together with questions for discussion and further research;

*   critical thinking activities designed to draw out the relevance of the chapter content to your own professional practice;

*   a conclusion and chapter reflections summarising content and learning points;

- suggestions for further reading headed 'Taking it further';
- references.

The case studies are based on real-life situations and are designed to be used either for individual study or as a stimulus for group discussion. In these studies you are asked to consider certain points, and hopefully to relate the situations to your own experience. There are no correct answers but you may find it useful to record your responses in a reflective journal.

The critical thinking activities are designed to help you consolidate and develop what you have learned. They encourage you to think about a particular aspect of the chapter and relate it to your own practice and to the theoretical concepts discussed in the chapter. They also give you the opportunity to research these concepts in relation to your own professional situation.

There are many terms in common use to describe teachers and learners: lecturer, trainer, tutor, instructor, student or service user come to mind. Normally this depends on where you are working, but for the purposes of this book the generic terms *teacher* and *learner* are used throughout, with the exception of verbatim quotations in the case studies and references.

How you use this book depends, to a large extent, on who you are and what you want from it. You may be a newly qualified teacher, a trainee working towards a teaching qualification, a teacher trainer or just someone with an interest in the subject. If you are in a teaching role, your teaching subject could be anything from accountancy to zoology. You may have many years of practical experience or have just started teaching. You will therefore want and need different things from your reading. If you are a trainee you may wish to work your way through the book. If you are an experienced teacher you might want to dip in, focusing on the chapters that interest you as an experienced professional. Not everyone, for example, will want to explore the political and historical context of professionalism outlined in Chapter 2. If you are a teacher trainer you might want to make use of some of the case studies and critical thinking activities to reinforce certain points or to consolidate your learners' learning.

And finally... can teaching be called the oldest profession? The female macaque monkey teaches its young to floss their teeth. The Arctic fox teaches its young to hunt. Parents pass on verbal language to their newborns. Clearly, teaching is a profession that is fundamental to the survival and ongoing success of a species; it is the most ancient of professions. To be part of this profession is something to be valued highly, and to participate in its activities is a powerful incentive for any teacher to aim for excellence.

References

LLUK (2007) *New Overarching Professional Standards for Teachers, Tutors and Trainers in the Lifelong Learning Sector*. London: LLUK.

2 Professionalism: protons, neutrons and electrons

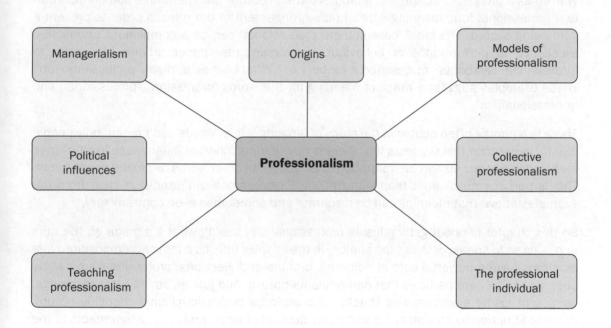

Managerialism

Origins

Models of professionalism

Political influences

Professionalism

Collective professionalism

Teaching professionalism

The professional individual

Chapter aims

This chapter will help you to:

- recognise the diverse nature of professionalism;

- understand how the concept of professionalism has developed over time;

- identify the impact of government policy on the nature of professionalism in general;

- identify the effects of government policy on professionalism in FE;

- identify the features of professionalism relevant to your professional role as an FE teacher.

Introduction

In his play *Mrs Warren's Profession,* George Bernard Shaw defined the character Kitty Warren as a professional; she was a brothel owner. Football commentators sometimes refer to a professional foul, meaning a deliberate infringement of the rules in order to prevent a goal being scored. The label 'consummate professional' can be a compliment to describe excellence in performance or behaviour. Conversely, newspaper articles may refer to 'professional layabouts', or describe a robbery or kidnapping as a 'highly professional job'. These examples suggest a range of meaning for the words 'profession', 'professional' and 'professionalism'.

There is a phrase often quoted in the study of language. It is 'Words don't mean, only people mean.' In essence this suggests that there is no meaning inherent in language itself; rather, meaning lies in our human interpretation of language. In other words, *we* make words mean. This is perhaps never truer than with the word 'professionalism', and it is clear from the examples above that meaning can be disparate and sometimes even contradictory.

So this chapter is about getting inside professionalism, seeing what it's made of, the nuts and bolts so to speak, or to use the analogy in the chapter title, its chemical composition. Just as atoms have a powerful core of neutrons, protons and electrons, professionalism can be seen as having core particles that determine its nature. And just as atoms react to change, gaining or losing electrons, this chapter also explores professionalism's changing nature, drawing attention to how meaning shifts and fluctuates when professionalism reacts to the dictates of society and political will. It reviews the range of interpretations of professionalism, and looks at how this can then be applied to teaching in FE.

What is professionalism?

CASE STUDY

Professional or not?

Glenys, Malcolm, Raul and Dennis are all currently working in the FE sector. Here are some brief details about each of them.

- Glenys is a retired primary school teacher who teaches t'ai chi at the local village hall on two evenings each week. She is an accredited t'ai chi instructor but does not get paid for her work.

- Malcolm is 35 with an HNC in Aeronautical Engineering. He is an RAF Chief Technician, and has been working as an instructor on the Aircraft Technician (Avionics) courses at the Defence College of Aeronautical Engineering for two years. His teaching qualification is the four-day RAF Instructional Technique course.

- Raul is an assistant manager at a large travel agency. He is also employed as a part-time teacher working for two hours each week on the BTEC Travel and Tourism course at his local FE college. He has 25 years' experience in the travel industry but has no teaching qualification.

- Dennis is 50, is not teacher trained but has a NEBOSH General Certificate in Occupational Health and Safety. He has worked for a large printing company all his working life, starting as a machine operator and progressing to the position of Safety Officer, which he has held for the past five years. He is responsible for teaching and managing all the Health and Safety courses offered by the firm for its employees.

Critical thinking activity

These personal details raise some interesting questions about professionalism.

» *Would you say that any or all of these four people are professional teachers?*

» *If not, why not?*

» *If they are, is their professionalism the same?*

» *What are the key criteria to determining whether they are professional or not?*

A good starting point to finding answers to these questions is to gain a clear idea of what professionalism actually means. The Oxford English dictionary states:

Professionalism: *noun*, the competence or skill expected of a professional: the key to quality and efficiency is professionalism.

Professional: *noun*, a person engaged or qualified in a profession: professionals such as lawyers and surveyors.

Profession: *noun*, paid occupation, especially one that involves prolonged training and a formal qualification: his chosen profession of teaching, a barrister by profession.

Combining these definitions, professionalism is the competence or skill of someone in a paid occupation, especially one that involves prolonged training and a formal qualification. This is all well and good but there are problems with the dictionary definitions. For one thing 'professionalism', 'professional' and 'profession' are over-used words; their meaning can become diluted or meaningless, or rather can have many different meanings for different people, making it difficult to get a handle on the concept as a basis for critical analysis. In many cases, these dictionary definitions can be far removed from much contemporary usage.

In order to gain a better understanding of professionalism, it is worthwhile exploring its origins and development.

Origins and historical context

Professionalism has its root in the Latin word 'profiteor', meaning to declare oneself within a religious context, such as belonging to a monastic order. This interpretation has the connotation of someone who is committed to a specific set of values and beliefs, a facet of professionalism that can be seen today in the various codes of ethics held by many professions. The Hippocratic Oath taken by doctors that requires them to swear to practise ethically and honestly is perhaps the best-known example.

At the start of the nineteenth century the title of 'profession' in Great Britain was the preserve of a very restricted number of occupations, notably the Church, the law and medicine. It was closely intertwined with the English class system whereby entry to one of these professions was an acceptable and high-status occupation for any upper class youth who needed to work for a living. This was in contrast to the lower status of a tradesman such as a carpenter or stonemason, even if the level of skill in such occupations was very high.

There were three dominant characteristics of these Victorian professions: specialist knowledge and skill, a code of ethics and a sense of vocation.

1.   *Specialist knowledge and skill* was gained through an extended period of training and guaranteed by success in a final examination and often some sort of probationary period. For example, the Law Society, founded in 1823 as the London Law Institution, delivered lectures and established an examination system, which is still the basis for solicitor training today.

2.   *A code of ethics and good practice* was guaranteed and enforced by an independent body. For instance, the General Medical Council, established in 1858, set standards for good medical practice and had the power to discipline any doctor who did not live up to these standards.

3.   *A sense of vocation* was encouraged so that those entering the profession did so primarily because of a love of the work itself, regardless of material reward. In this sense, a profession is a calling, particularly evident in those who joined the clergy.

As the nineteenth century progressed, a trend emerged for an increasing number of occupations to establish a professional status; in other words to professionalise. Many of these occupations were connected to the Industrial Revolution, with the Institution of Mechanical Engineers being founded in 1847 and the Institution of Electrical Engineers being established in 1871. Others were essentially administrative professions such as accountancy, with the Institute of Accountants being formed in Edinburgh in 1853.

These occupational groups based their professional structure on the experience of the traditional professions with an emphasis on the acquisition of a core of specialised knowledge, obtained through a period of training, organised and licensed by a central body. This became a public guarantee of expertise and a high standard of ethics and professional behaviour. Finally, there was an assumption of a high level of motivation, of a love of professional work for its own sake rather than material reward. The result was an increasing number of occupations calling themselves professional. They were self-regulating, enjoyed high status and tended towards exclusivity.

So far so good. Traditional professionalism in the United Kingdom (UK) at the start of the twentieth century was a concept readily understood and fairly easy to define. These high-status and exclusive organisations provided a model for other aspirational occupations. However, things were to become more complex. As the twentieth century progressed, a whole raft of occupations perceived an advantage in professional status and aspired to a similar standing in society. For these occupations – nursing, management, social work, librarianship and many more – professionalisation became a strategic objective. The motivation was partially to seek an increase in status, partially to gain influence against bureaucratic and political pressure, and also to serve their service users more effectively.

Different occupations have professionalised in different ways. In nursing for example, much emphasis has been placed on ensuring that specialist knowledge is of a high standard. Thus, nurse training was transferred to the higher education (HE) sector as far back as 1985, and currently the minimum academic award for nursing programmes in the UK is a degree. Management now has a professional body, the Chartered Management Institute, to represent the interests of the profession. Since the 1960s, MBAs have been offered in the UK and have become a major feature in the education and training of senior managers. Priorities in the professionalisation process were being determined by the occupation's interpretation of the nature of professionalism.

The nature of professionalism: corporate professionalism

Any occupational group seeking to redefine itself as professional needs a clear idea about what a profession actually is. Many occupational groups start from the standpoint of looking at the classic professions such as medicine and law, and transferring what they see as the key features of these professions to their own occupation. Others turn to academic scholarship to gain a better understanding of an ideal model of a professional organisation.

They are not short of material, as a plethora of academic models contribute to this debate. One of the more popular approaches is known as the trait model, which defines the criteria to judge whether an occupation can be deemed as professional or not. One such model was put forward by Geoffrey Millerson in 1964 and it defined six key features of professionalism:

1. a skill based on theoretical knowledge;
2. intellectual education and training;
3. the testing of competence;
4. closure of the profession by restrictive organisation;
5. a code of professional conduct;
6. an altruistic service to the 'public good'.

There are more recent models based on similar lists of criteria, such as Cyril Houle's model in 1980 and Donald Belfall's model in 1999. All such models are slightly different but with considerable overlap in their criteria.

These trait models provided emergent professions with a route map that could be used to chart progress to professional recognition, but they have attracted a fair bit of criticism. For example, the lists of traits seem arbitrary. Why focus on certain traits rather than others? Furthermore, could such a model be realistically applied to professional individuals as well as occupational groups?

Critical thinking activity: defining 'profession'

» *What are the advantages and limitations of trait models in determining whether an occupational group is professional or not?*
» *To what extent does the contemporary FE sector meet Millerson's criteria of professionalism?*
» *Can you identify other models that are more appropriate?*

The nature of professionalism: the professional individual

The notion of being a professional individual is just as complex as that of a professional organisation. Consider for a moment the definition of a professional as someone who is paid, as distinct from amateurs who gain no material reward from their activity.

Amateur versus *professional*

The modern Olympic Games, first held in Athens in 1896, were a celebration of the amateur ideal – excellence motivated solely by love of the sport with no material reward – in contrast to professional athletes who were paid for their performances. This perception of professionalism, which permeated British sport early in the twentieth century, implied that the amateur had greater value and status than the professional. Rugby Union, played by amateurs, was the preserve of the educated upper and middle classes; Rugby League was the working-class professional game rooted in the industrial north of England. First-class cricket matches between amateur and professional players, named Gentlemen v Players, were held until 1962. Can you guess which team was called 'Gentlemen'?

Nowadays, the status of amateur vis-à-vis professional has pretty much reversed. To be called amateur is almost an insult, implying shoddy workmanship; for instance, 'amateur night at the opera' is a cliché denoting a low standard of performance. By contrast, professionalism now indicates excellence, commitment and a lot of money. Gold medals in twenty-first century Olympic Games are won by professional athletes who have given years of their life preparing for an event that comes once every four years. Rigidly controlled diets and training regimes totally dominate the lives of these professionals. If the original meaning of profession meant giving your life to God by going into a monastery, this total commitment to world-class excellence is perhaps the modern-day equivalent.

This interpretation of professionalism – commitment, excellence and reward – has now permeated other occupations not usually associated with being a profession. Here is Steve, a self-employed painter and decorator, talking about his work.

CASE STUDY

Steve

Professional? Of course I'm a professional; I get paid and I'm good at my job. After school I went to college and got an NVQ2 in P and D, worked for my uncle for a while and four years ago set up on my own. I've never looked back, and that's because I take pride in what I do. You wouldn't believe some of the rubbish I come across when I first go into some houses; cowboy jobs, cheap paint that has run and flaked, no real preparation so the surfaces are rough and lumpy, paint splashes around window edges. I'm not cheap, but I do a quality job and word gets round. I've never had to advertise, it's all word of mouth and I've got a two-month waiting list. I give a good service to my customers; turn up on time, do what I promise, work hard while I'm on a job and take a lot of care cleaning up. I think this is all part of being professional.

Critical thinking activity

» *Would you say this description of professionalism is appropriate to you as a professional FE teacher? Give reasons for your opinion.*

Steve's description of professionalism could apply to a wide range of jobs, rather than just a few high-status occupations. You don't have to belong to a profession to be professional. The essential criteria are:

- expert knowledge and skill, gained through training and practice;
- a commitment to improvement and excellence;
- a commitment to providing a good service to others;
- commensurate reward.

Knowledge, autonomy and responsibility

As you have seen, the trait models of professionalism may be useful to occupations seeking to professionalise, but for individuals these models tend to be restrictive and inflexible. A more appropriate approach was formulated by Eric Hoyle and Peter John in 1995. They define professionalism in terms of three inter-related and fundamental concepts: knowledge, autonomy and responsibility.

1. *Specialised knowledge* is seen as the basis of professional practice. It is underpinned by an understanding of the relevant theory and is validated by application in practice. Such knowledge is usually acquired through rigorous and demanding training.

2. *Autonomy* is a consequence of attaining this knowledge and understanding. Professional judgements often need to be made in unpredictable situations, and professionals need to be able to make these judgements to respond to the needs of their service users free from bureaucratic and political restriction.

3. *Responsibility* is owed to service users, employers and to society in general. These groups need to be confident that the professional is committed to a comprehensive and clear set of values that provides an ethical basis for professional activity.

To see how these three elements might apply in practice, consider Yasmin, a social worker, talking about her work.

CASE STUDY

Yasmin

Social work sometimes gets a bad press and you seldom hear of the success stories, but I'm actually very proud of being a social worker and I believe I do a professional job.

It took considerable training and hard work to get where I am, and so I really value that piece of paper stating that I am qualified. I work with families who are mostly struggling with various problems of one sort or another. I work as part of a team – we liaise on a daily basis, and of course, anything that I'm the slightest bit doubtful about I discuss with another member of the team, but at the same time I am very conscious of my individual responsibility towards each of the families I work with.

Take something like setting boundaries so as not to get too drawn into the family's problems. You want to help the family you are working with, this is why you do social work, but it's easy to get drawn in. Imagine a cotton thread tying you to the family, one thread you hardly notice, but as the threads increase there is a danger you become caught up. This isn't good for you. And it's certainly not good for the family because you are going to have to withdraw at some point and understandably the family may then feel let down. So it's important for us to be able to manage boundaries in a professional manner. We get training and support but at the end of the day it's your decision where that line is drawn.

Critical thinking activity

» *How would you say Yasmin's description of her work illustrates professionalism in the context of knowledge, autonomy and responsibility?*

One significant limitation to the models of professionalism discussed so far is that they do not take into account the importance of the political and economic context. Governments, stakeholders and the economic environment have a major influence on the nature and status of occupations.

The nature of professionalism: the political agenda

An important influence in the current understanding of professionalism is the view of the political establishment and society at large. The days of professions automatically being accorded deference and respect are long gone, if they ever existed. Until the middle of the last century, professional autonomy was generally accepted as long as the professions were perceived to be acting in the interests of their service users and society as a whole. On occasion, however, they were seen to be pursuing their own benefit at the expense of society behind the protection of unaccountable professional bodies – what George Bernard Shaw (1856–1950) termed 'the conspiracy against the laity'. Professions have consequently come under increasing scrutiny, particularly by governments claiming to be acting in the public interest.

Political interest and involvement in the activities of professional occupations has its basis in the desire for accountability, particularly in those sectors providing a public service such as health and education. In the 1970s there was a trend under Labour administrations to make the professions more accountable, and Margaret Thatcher accelerated this trend with enthusiasm when she became Conservative Prime Minister. One good example of this was her education policy in the 1980s. The government was determined to wrest control of education from the educational establishment, that is the teaching profession. The National Curriculum was introduced, with attainment tested through Standard Assessment Tests (SATs) at the end of each key stage. Teacher training was subject to greater central control through the Council for the Accreditation of Teacher Education (CATE). Combined with other measures that gave greater power to parents and governors, the effect was to change the nature of school teacher professionalism, essentially by increasing regulation and restricting autonomy.

This policy of increasing central control of professional groups has proceeded apace since the Thatcher years and shows no sign of slowing down. It is characterised by the introduction of regulatory bodies, control of professional training, nationally defined standards, monitoring of performance through inspection and the power to penalise those professionals who provide inadequate service. This is a political agenda that encourages the professions to operate as efficiently as possible to support economic and social policy. One consequence of this development is the increase of managerialism, the need for a separate management function in those sectors that have felt the impact of government regulation.

The purpose of management in this context is to make professional organisations as efficient as possible by planning, administering and evaluating the service provided in the most effective way possible. The NHS provides a good example of this trend. The 2010 NHS census (HSCIC, 2011) recorded an 84 per cent increase in the number of managers between 1999 and 2010 and also noted the effect of this increase on clinical professionals. Between 2009 and 2010 the number of managers increased by 11.9 per cent, while the number of nurses increased by less than 2 per cent and consultants by less than 6 per cent. Clearly the political agenda was exerting a major influence on the relationship between professional and managerial elements in the NHS, and this has implications for education and FE.

Professionalism in FE

Are you a professional? Do you work in a professional occupational group? The answers to these questions depend on the theoretical model of professionalism that you care to choose. When you measured your job against Millerson's model you may have found some areas of doubt, such as the criterion of the profession being subject to a restrictive organisation. Measured against Steve, the decorator's model, the answer is almost certainly yes. Clearly there is a material reward, although the current disadvantage of salary level when compared with school teachers' salary structure is a sensitive issue. Most would agree that within the FE sector there is an ethos of providing a good service to others together with a commitment to improvement and high-quality work. But things are more complex than this. You need to look at how the political agenda has impacted on the nature of professionalism in the sector and the teachers working within it – firstly, corporate professionalism in FE.

Managerial professionalism

For the last quarter of a century successive British governments have sought to increase their control and influence in the education system, not least in the post-16 sector. Not an easy task when you consider the diversity and ambiguous status of the sector, with FE seen as the inbetween service, between schools on the one hand and HE or the world of work on the other. The cliché most frequently used is to call FE 'the Cinderella service', which brings to mind an overworked and exploited service but with a potential for great things if only Prince Charming would come along and fit the appropriate slipper. Then FE would be seen as a truly professional sector and take its place as an equal partner to the schools and HE sectors. Prime candidates for the Prince Charming role over the past 25 years or so are the successive governments who have wished to promote FE as a professional service, essentially as a service provider, preparing people for work.

Governments have spent considerable time and money to attain this ambition. This is an unusual situation. Traditionally, emergent professions organised themselves to gain professional recognition, particularly by the government of the day. The professions themselves designed, delivered and assessed training. They formulated codes of ethics and practice, and created independent bodies to enforce these codes. These independent bodies sought to represent their occupational groups to government and to society as a whole. This applies not only to well-established professions, such as the Law Society representing solicitors and the British Medical Association (BMA) representing doctors, but also to new occupational groups like information technology (IT) workers. In 2006, in order to validate a professional model, the British Computer Society commissioned a research project that analysed the way seven established professions operated (BCS, 2006). A key feature of this report was that the profession should speak with a single voice and offer a co-ordinated view to government and industry.

FE has not been so proactive and representation to government has been fragmented, involving a mixture of trade unions like the University and College Union (UCU), local authorities, awarding organisations and so forth. Governments have increasingly intervened, seeing professional FE as an essential element in producing a trained and effective workforce upon which the economic prosperity of the nation depends. If the FE sector was unable to professionalise itself, the government would do it for them.

Incorporation of colleges

A key event in this process was the passing of the Further and Higher Education Act in 1992, which freed FE colleges from local authority control and gave them the status of independent corporations with control of their own budgets. Prior to this, local authorities had been the major influence in the development of FE provision through their responsibility to provide 'adequate facilities for Further Education' under the terms of the 1944 Education Act. The result was that by the 1980s over 500 colleges were delivering programmes reflecting local authority priorities, culture and politics. It is not surprising that there was massive variation in quality and scope. The 1992 Act was intended to liberate colleges from a public sector control that was seen by the Thatcher administration as pedestrian, unresponsive and divorced from the real world.

As a consequence, traditional general FE colleges have found themselves operating in a very different environment well summarised by Roy Fisher and Robin Simmons, who describe the FE sector as

> a mixed economy of semi-privatised state sector organisations alongside a plethora of state-subsidised private sector providers. Institutions formerly having a public sector ethos are now expected to behave like private businesses; performance indicators are set; funding is tied to targets and managerialism is commonplace. Education is regarded as a commodity that can be provided cheaply and efficiently by organisations imbued with an ideology of enterprise.
>
> (Avis et al., 2010, p 8)

Local authority control had emphasised co-operation between colleges. For example, in large cities local colleges were encouraged to specialise in particular curriculum areas rather than compete for enrolments from a limited pool of potential learners. That has all changed. Competition between colleges has replaced the pre-1992 co-operative ethos, and the results are striking. Some colleges have closed or been merged with more powerful neighbours. Others have prospered, and now possess impressive new buildings and equipment, high-profile marketing departments and all the other signs of a successful business. The business-centred approach has markedly affected FE teachers. New contracts, increased teaching hours, more administration and more demanding conditions of service have been the inevitable consequence of the increased emphasis on funding and cost saving. Those of your colleagues who worked in an FE college prior to 1992 may well regale you with tales of a halcyon age when FE teachers taught for 21 hours each week in a 38-week year and went on six-week summer holidays abroad.

As the sector became more entrepreneurial, successive governments implemented a process to professionalise the workforce. Specifically, this meant ensuring that all FE teachers were trained In teaching skills, held a licence to practise, were members of a professional body and were committed to their own professional development throughout their teaching career. Professional standards that defined the knowledge and skills that FE teachers needed to possess were introduced in 2001. Traditional qualifications for FE teachers such as the Certificate in Education (Cert Ed) and Postgraduate Certificate in Education (PGCE) were modified to ensure that these standards were covered in the curriculum design of these qualifications.

Development of professional teaching standards

The process of establishing mandatory professional standards for FE teachers culminated with the introduction of the 2007 regulations for the FE sector. These standards, designed and monitored by Lifelong Learning UK (LLUK) defined the values and standards of practice expected from a professional FE teacher. An extract from the section on professional values is detailed in Appendix A. The standards formed the basis for a three-level qualification structure to be offered either as stand-alone qualifications or embedded within existing PGCEs or Cert Eds. This was the foundation of the training and testing of teacher competence that the government saw as a key characteristic of professionalism. All FE teachers would need to hold an appropriate teaching qualification as a pre-requisite of gaining the status of Qualified Teacher Learning and Skills (QTLS) or Associate Teacher Learning and Skills (ATLS): their licence to practise.

Another government requirement under the 2007 regulations was that FE teachers continue to develop their knowledge and skills throughout their career – CPD. Thus the regulations included a requirement that FE teachers, in order to maintain their licence, should undertake and provide evidence of at least 30 hours of CPD in any one year. The instrument for managing this process, alongside the responsibility for awarding QTLS and ATLS status, was entrusted to the Institute for Learning (IfL), which was intended to be the sector's professional regulatory body. As such, it would have a similar role to that of the Law Society for solicitors or the BMA for doctors and represent the FE sector to government, stakeholders, service users and society as a whole. The IfL would define membership requirements, issue a licence to practise, establish a universally accepted code of conduct and generally fulfil the roles traditionally undertaken by other professional bodies.

This top-down approach to establishing a professional FE teaching service was modified in 2012, with official acceptance that over-prescriptive regulation may compromise professionalism rather than encourage it. Hence the mandatory aspects of the 2007 regulations were revoked. The requirement for all FE teachers to hold QTLS or ATLS status and be members of the IfL was still to be encouraged but was no longer mandatory. The aim was that, with the formation of the Education and Training Foundation (ETF) as a professional body to represent the sector, FE teachers and other stakeholders in the sector would have greater influence in the shape of FE in the future.

Effects of managerialism

It is clear that government policy following the incorporation of colleges has led to an increase in managerialism, similar to that in the NHS. This has had a significant impact on the work of teachers within the sector and can be illustrated by the story of Basheer, who served as a member of a medium-sized college's senior management team before and after 1993. Here he describes how his role within his college has changed since incorporation.

CASE STUDY

Basheer

I don't think we appreciated the difference incorporation and government regulation would make to the character of the college. Before incorporation, nearly all the senior management team were academics – lecturers who had been promoted to management positions. We'd learned management by experience as curriculum leaders or as departmental heads, and our credibility was based on our experience as teachers. We really understood what it was like to teach in ill-equipped classrooms, to deal with disruptive classes and to cope with awkward parents and employers because we'd done it for years.

But within three years of incorporation, the SMT was very different. Most of the members had never taught in a classroom – a finance director who was an ACCA qualified accountant, an HR director who was a member of the CIPD, a resource director who had been an estates manager for a pharmaceutical company, and so on. They were all expert professionals in their field and knew the technicalities backwards. But I don't think they understood FE, and just regarded students as some sort of commodity that would bring funding to the college.

Critical thinking activity: the nature of professionalism in FE

»   *What effect do you think the increase in managerialism has had on FE institutions since incorporation?*

»   *The preferred model of the state... construes the FE teacher as a service provider, at the behest of the market, one who will acquire earned autonomy as a 'trusted servant' of the state... lecturers feel casualised and deprofessionalised by a process of market, funding-led and managerialist reform.*

(Avis et al., 2010, p 42)

»   *To what extent is Avis' analysis of FE teacher professionalism an accurate reflection of the current situation in the sector? Justify your judgement with reference to government reform, relevant literature and personal experience.*

Democratic professionalism in FE

The introduction of mandatory teaching qualifications and compulsory membership of the IfL, introduced with the 2007 regulations for FE teachers, encountered significant opposition from the sector, culminating in a fees dispute in 2009. The limitations of imposing professionalism by government mandate were recognised in the Lingfield report

> *the sector has been 'infantilised and encumbered' by too much and too detailed intervention by government and its agencies. It seems to us likely that these interventions have, in the name of control and accountability, weakened the very characteristics successive governments have wished to nourish: good governance; self-reliance in academic quality assurance and continuous improvement; and a primary focus on furthering the interests of customers – students, their employers and their communities.*

(BIS, 2012, p 1)

The Lingfield report acknowledged the problems associated with a top-down approach to imposing a professional structure by mandate and advocated a different strategy. This was founded on establishing a more democratic profession where the members had a sense of ownership and there was a genuine dialogue between the profession, its stakeholders and its service users – learners, employers, government, universities and so on. To do this, the sector needed strong representation through a central body, which would be accepted and owned by the sector rather than being imposed on it. Hence the proposal to establish the ETF. All this, of course, has considerable implications for the professionalism of teachers working in the sector.

The professional individual in FE

From your point of view as an individual teacher, whether or not FE is labelled as a profession is probably not of world-shattering importance. But government regulation certainly matters, because it directly affects how you enter post-16 teaching, how you operate on a day-to-day basis and how you progress through your career. To gain some insight into the effect of these developments on the professionalism of an FE teacher today, you may find it useful to consider the work of Hoyle and John (1995). They saw individual professionalism as comprising three inter-related strands: specialised knowledge, autonomy and responsibility.

Specialised knowledge

For any FE teacher, specialised knowledge has two elements. The first is the subject knowledge that you bring to your work as a teacher. This may be a degree in sociology, 20 years' experience working as a restaurant chef, an advanced engineering qualification or experience and qualifications in any of the FE subject areas. In all cases it is the basis of your professional practice and confers credibility and authority when facing a lively group of learners. This knowledge is underpinned by an understanding of subject theory that needs to be current and constantly updated. In this sense, you are clearly a professional, but a professional subject specialist rather than a professional teacher.

If you want to be a professional teacher, in addition to subject expertise you need specialised knowledge of teaching, normally gained through a combination of a teaching qualification and experience of practical teaching. So you need to be a professional twice over – first in your specialist subject, second as a professional teacher. There can be tensions in this situation. For example, your expectations based on your experience as a professional in your main discipline may not match the reality of your role as a teacher. Here is Clare describing her baptism into teaching insurance in an FE college.

CASE STUDY

Clare

Before I went into teaching I was in the insurance industry. I began my working life in a large marine and general insurance company, moving around the company to gain experience. I then spent a number of years working for an insurance broker. At this point, together with a colleague, I set up an independent commercial insurance brokerage specialising in factory, office and retail insurance. Circumstances then dictated a change in my career. The company my husband worked for relocated, we moved and my insurance career came to an end. I saw this as an opportunity to pass on the business skills I'd learned on the job in my years in a service industry and began working in the School of Business and Finance at my local FE college.

As a broker I'd prided myself on my professional approach to my work. If a service user had a problem that needed sorting I would drop everything and go and sort it out. In fact we had an unwritten law 'If the service user says jump, we jump.' To be honest we saw ourselves very much in the role of servants; if we didn't provide an excellent service the service user would go elsewhere and because each service user account represented a substantial fee any loss would seriously affect the business. So there was always this metaphorical stick. The carrot of course was expansion of the business and our own pride in a job well done. I think the majority of good businesses operate like this regardless of whether the business is a sole trading plumber or a large firm of accountants.

When I went into FE teaching the character of professionalism for me changed. Basically there was no longer any recognisable stick. Don't get me wrong, clearly there are consequences when teaching is mediocre but that ever-present requirement to produce excellence all the time or woe betide your next pay packet had evaporated. I soon came to understand that as far as teaching is concerned professionalism means offering the best service to learners solely for the sake of offering the best service. In other words it's far more to do with what's operating inside you rather than what's happening around you.

Critical thinking activity

»   *Would you say your professional approach to your work changed when you moved from your main discipline into teaching and, if so, how?*

Autonomy

Autonomy is one of the features of professionalism that has long been prized by teachers. At one level it involves the judgements that have to be made in the unpredictable classroom situations that arise on a daily basis. In a more general sense it involves a claim that teachers should determine the curriculum, as was often the case with those lecturers who taught General Studies in the 1960s and 1970s. Duncan describes his experience in a large FE college.

CASE STUDY

Duncan

I started working in a college in 1972, as a lecturer in General Studies. It was a real eye opener.

Before this I'd been doing odd jobs – bar work, helping my brother in his garden centre, a stint in a food processing factory and so on. This was after I'd finished my degree in sociology and done a C & G 730 teaching certificate part time, which had fired up my ambition to become a professional teacher in FE. I arrived in my new job with a lot of idealism and maybe I could pass this on to the students. A rude awakening was in store.

Most of my classes were composed of lads on part-time day release who had been sent by their employers to get qualified in their trade – bricklayers, welders, motor vehicle mechanics. General Studies was an hour on their timetable each week that was meant to give an extra dimension to the course, to make them better citizens as it were. OK in theory, problematic in practice.

The first shock was that my students didn't want to know; to them, General Studies was a waste of time when they could otherwise have been taking car engines to bits or whatever, or better still going to the pub. A bit of a culture change from the A-level sociology students I'd met on teaching practice!

So initially it was a survival exercise. Hours and hours spent thinking of things that would grab the students' interest, planning activities that would keep them busy, talking to the vocational teachers about what topics I could teach that would be useful to them, negotiating with reluctant and truculent students.

On the other hand, it was a luxury being able to teach the things I felt were important. The general attitude seemed to be, 'Teach what you like as long as the students don't cause problems for anyone else!' So I did a whole term on the Industrial Revolution and how conditions of work had changed for workers since then, so that they could understand the context of their work. We had some really lively discussions, particularly when we got on to trade unions. I'm not sure one or two of their employers were over-impressed with this part of the college course they were paying for!

It's different now. Standards, objectives, outcomes, assessment and all that were noticeably absent from my life as a General Studies lecturer. But I reckon I did a good professional job once I learned how to survive in an atmosphere reminiscent of Wilt in Tom Sharpe's novels. My abiding memory is of Jimmy, one of the most awkward lads in the welding class who came up to me at the end of the course to tell me he was going to enrol in a sociology evening class. He eventually went on to do A level. It made all the tribulations worthwhile really.

Critical thinking activity

Duncan says that he did a good professional job.

»   *What evidence is there for this claim?*

»   *How valid is his version of professionalism today?*

As Duncan says, 'It's different now'. FE teachers rarely make these curriculum judgements free from bureaucratic and political restriction. The 'teach what you like' attitude that Duncan experienced is very much a thing of the past. One paradoxical effect of the political thrust to make the FE sector more professional by regulation has been to reduce the role of teachers as autonomous experts, and strengthen their role as providing a service in line with political priorities.

Responsibility

The flip side of autonomy is responsibility; this is the price you pay for your individual freedom of action and it is linked to your professional values. Jocelyn Robson expresses this succinctly:

> It is precisely because individual practitioners have the opportunity to decide and to make choices and judgments about best courses of action that they have responsibilities to act well and in accordance with their professional values.
>
> (Robson, 2006, p 19)

Each of us has a set of professional values that guide our professional behaviour. Most of us have an image of an excellent teacher, how they behave and how they relate to their learners and colleagues. This may be a teacher who has changed your life in some way and has become a role model that you would like to emulate. Or you may have been influenced by writers, or by watching a colleague at work. Your philosophy of teaching is likely to stem from experiences such as these; they determine your professional value system and your view of professionalism.

Governments have not been slow to spell out the responsibilities of teachers in terms of desired professional values, with the focus on teacher responsibility towards the learner. Consequently, the 2007 LLUK professional standards and values are very much learner focused. As the introduction states:

> Teachers in the lifelong learning sector value all learners individually and equally... The key purpose of the teacher is to create effective and stimulating opportunities for learning through high quality teaching that enables the development and progression of all learners.
>
> (LLUK, 2007, p 2)

Your professional values and responsibilities are applicable to a much broader context than daily classroom management. They apply to your relationships with the wide group of people who have expectations of a professional service from you: employers, parents, colleagues, exam boards to name but a few. These groups need to be confident that any professional teacher holds a clear set of values that provide a basis for trust and respect. There is also the responsibility to develop your professional skills throughout your career. Initially it is likely that the emphasis will be on attaining teaching skills, but your development needs will change as your career advances. Once your teaching skills have been consolidated, your professional development will increasingly be based on a sophisticated self-evaluation of your needs.

This regulatory approach of setting standards for good practice and ensuring the professionalism of FE teachers is also evident in the IfL code of professional practice that outlines the ethical basis of its members' professional behaviour (Appendix B). Under the headings of integrity, respect, care, practice, disclosure and responsibility the code details how it expects a professional FE teacher to behave. The phraseology of this code reflects its regulatory background with phrases such as 'in accordance with relevant legislation and organisational requirements'. It also outlines sanctions that can be imposed on any member not living up to these standards, progressing from reprimand through to expulsion.

Critical thinking activity: professional values

» *How would you define your professional values as a teacher? Compare your conclusions to the professional values listed in Domain A of the 2007 LLUK Standards and to your initial analysis of professionalism that was the focus of the first case study at the start of this chapter.*

» *To what extent does the IfL code of professional practice reflect your personal values and standards for your professional practice?*

» *What are the advantages and limitations of such a code being mandatory for your profession?*

Conclusion: professionalism in FE

This chapter has made a distinction between corporate professionalism (where an occupational group sets standards for its members) and individual professionalism (where an individual has their own vision of what it means to be a professional). From now on, the focus will be on this latter concept – specifically on you as a professional teacher in contemporary FE.

One thing is obvious from this discussion on the nature of professionalism: it is a difficult term to define with precision. But there is considerable common ground in all the models looked at. Just as atoms have a powerful nucleus composed of protons and neutrons that endures over time, there are some core features of teaching professionalism that seem to endure:

• subject expertise – the knowledge base;

• teaching expertise – excellence in practice underpinned by theory;

• continuing learning – curiosity and enthusiasm for both subject and teaching;

• autonomy in the management of learning;

• multiple accountability: to learners, organisations, service users, society;

• acceptance of a code of ethics and practice.

Attaining this status is not easy. It requires a high level of self-awareness, understanding of others, effective relationships with learners, a high level of teaching skills and being an effective member of the organisation. These are areas to be explored in the following chapters.

Chapter reflections

» *There is a range of interpretations of the word 'professionalism'.*

» *These interpretations change and develop over time, responding to economic and political change.*

» *There is a common core to professionalism that includes specialised knowledge and skill obtained through training, ethical principles, guaranteed standards of excellence, continuous development, autonomy and responsibility.*

»   *FE has been subject to government regulation to professionalise, with the introduction of professional standards, qualifications and mandatory CPD; one consequence of regulation has been to reduce teacher autonomy.*

»   *Professional values are the basis for the professionalism of FE teachers.*

Taking it further

Armitage, A, Bryant, R, Dunnill, R, Flanagan, K, Hayes, D, Hudson, A, Kent, J, Lawes, S and Renwick, M (2007) *Teaching and Training in Post-Compulsory Education*. Maidenhead: McGraw Hill.
This book serves as a general introduction to teacher professionalism within FE. It contains comprehensive chapters on political developments concerning the sector and on professional development.

Avis, J, Fisher, R and Simmons, R (2009) *Issues in Post-Compulsory Education and Training: Critical Perspectives*. Huddersfield: University of Huddersfield Press.
This is a series of papers on contemporary FE, including history, government policy, professionalism and managerialism.

Cole, M (2008) *Professional Attributes and Practice*. Abingdon: Routledge.
Although aimed at teacher professionalism in schools, this book gives a comprehensive and accessible review of the nature of professionalism issues and provides practical advice to help student teachers and teachers prepare for their professional life.

Hoyle, E and John, P (1995) *Professional Knowledge and Professional Practice*. London: Cassell.
This is a comprehensive analysis of the nature of individual professionalism.

Wallace, S (2013) *Understanding the Further Education Sector*. Northwich: Critical Publishing.

References

Avis, J, Fisher, R and Ollin, R (2010) Professionalism, in Avis, J, Fisher, R and Thompson, P (eds) *Teaching in Lifelong Learning: A Guide to Theory and Practice*. Buckingham: Open University Press.

BCS (2006) *Report on the Study of Established Professions to Validate the IT Professionalism Model*. Swindon: British Computer Society.

Belfall, D (1999) *Creating Value for Members*. Toronto: Canadian Society for Association Executives.

BIS (Oct 2012) *Professionalism in Further Education – Final Report*. London: BIS.

Houle, C (1980) *Continuing Learning in the Professions*. San Francisco: Jossey-Bass.

Hoyle, E and John, P (1995) *Professional Knowledge and Professional Practice*. London: Cassell.

HSCIC (2011) *NHS Workforce: Summary of Staff in the NHS: Results from September 2010 Census*. London: Health and Social Care Information Centre.

LLUK (2007) *New Overarching Professional Standards for Teachers, Tutors and Trainers in the Lifelong Learning Sector*. London: LLUK.

Millerson, G (1964) *The Qualifying Associations: A Study in Professionalization*. London: Routledge.

Robson, J (2006) *Teacher Professionalism in Further and Higher Education*. London: Routledge.

Websites

www.aoc.co.uk (last accessed 6 February 2014)
www.bis.gov.uk/assets/BISCore/further-education-skills (last accessed 6 February 2014)
www.et-foundation.co.uk (last accessed 6 February 2014)
www.ifl.ac.uk (last accessed 6 February 2014)

3 Upfront and personal: the merits of self-absorption

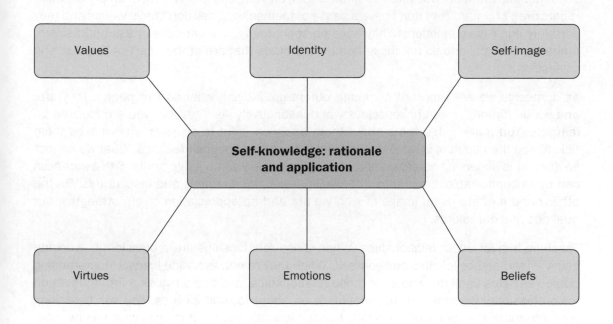

Chapter aims

This chapter will help you to:

*   understand the nature of professional identity;

*   understand the role of values, virtues and emotions in your interactions with others;

*   define your educational philosophy.

Introduction

Imagine for a moment a scenario in which robot teachers have been programmed to plan and deliver perfect lessons. It should sound like a good idea but you know it isn't. So what's wrong with this futuristic scenario? It's glaringly obvious of course, that no matter how sophisticated the programming, robots can't reason; they are not able to think on their feet, to be flexible, to adapt and to respond to learners and to the unexpected that can arise in any teaching situation. But you also know intuitively that this is a bad idea simply *because* robots aren't human. They don't have a sense of themselves, they don't have values and they certainly don't have emotions. They have no spontaneity, and cannot express enthusiasm, empathy, curiosity and so on, those human attributes that are at the heart of the teaching profession.

As a species we are expert at summing others up, judging what sort of person they are, and we do it more or less unconsciously and instinctively. As a teacher you are focused on learners. You make judgements about them and work hard to discover what makes them tick, to see their point of view, to understand their values and their feelings. What we are not so good at is observing ourselves and making those very same judgements. Self-awareness can be uncomfortable; it can throw up weaknesses, uncertainties and insecurities. On the other hand it offers us an image of who we are and an appreciation of our strengths, our qualities and our talents.

Teaching is a lot about relationships. When those relationships are professional, everyone gains – learners, colleagues and yourself. When they're not, everyone loses. Understanding ourselves helps to oil the wheels of those relationships, and this provides a firm foundation for professional practice. So this chapter is all about looking inwards. You will be asking yourself some questions which relate to your identity, your self-image, your values, your beliefs and your emotional responses to others.

Identity

In the children's storybook, *Alice's Adventures in Wonderland,* by Lewis Carroll, Alice asks, 'Who in the world am I? Ah, that's the great puzzle'. And this question that Alice poses seems a reasonable starting point to explore what is meant by identity. If you were asked to describe who you were you might say that you were a teacher, full time or part time, that you worked in FE or HE or in industry, commerce or public services. You might say that you were a graduate, that you were doing an MA or that you had a specialist vocational skill and/or experience.

One or more of these statements might be a pretty accurate description of yourself but it is unlikely that you would see any of them as your identity.

The doleful Jacques in Shakespeare's play *As You Like It* utters the famous words, 'All the world's a stage, and all the men and women merely players; they have their exits and their entrances; and one man in his time plays many parts'. Shakespeare is likening life to a play and we, the actors, play a host of parts in the play, changing costumes with each part. The parts that we act out are the different roles we take up in our everyday lives such as teacher, employee, colleague and so on. For each role there is an expectation of certain behaviour or action. The expected behaviour for a learner, for example, is very different from that of a teacher. As a teacher you have certain ways of behaving that you share with your colleagues and that learners and colleagues alike can expect from you. These roles are temporary; you inhabit them for a period of time and move on. None of them represents the real you. So 'teacher', while describing one of your roles, is not indicative of your identity.

Identity differs from role in that it is more fundamental to who you are rather than something you move in and out of, and it encompasses your personal values and beliefs. Professional identity has been described as

> *a set of externally ascribed attributes that differentiate one group from another... imposed upon the teaching profession either by outsiders or by members of the teaching fraternity itself.*
>
> (Sachs, 2011, p 124)

Your professional identity may be one that is imposed but it is mediated by your personal values and experience and develops through your relationships with others. Defining identity, Etienne Wenger suggests that, 'who we are lies in the way we live day to day not just in what we think or say about ourselves' (Wenger, 1998 p 151). Note how this happens through the experience of one teacher, Jay, whose professional identity was modified through his experience and his relationships with his learners and his colleagues.

CASE STUDY

Jay's shift in identity

I originally trained as an acupuncturist and after qualifying I spent four years in China gaining more experience of both acupuncture techniques and Chinese medicine. When I returned to the UK I set up my own acupuncture clinic taking on a number of practitioners as the business expanded. I began teaching a number of years ago initially on a part-time basis, but I now teach acupuncture and Chinese medicine more or less full time.

As a professional acupuncturist with my own business I was pretty much autonomous. My employees tended to look to me for guidance and I had a reputation with patients as a very good practitioner. I knew as soon as I began teaching that it was something I really wanted to continue with but I had brought with me this notion of myself as the font of all knowledge and thought that my students would respond in much the same way as patients.

Early on I was reluctant to accept advice and guidance from colleagues or to share ideas with them. I valued my autonomy, believed that I was the authority and had little to learn from those around me. When it was suggested to me that I might find it helpful to pair up with an experienced teacher I resisted at first. But Conchita was really supportive. I had the opportunity to watch her in action and began to learn from her, to see how she was always open to opinions and ideas and how she appeared to have a relaxed and genuine relationship with both her students and her colleagues.

Gradually it became apparent to me that OK, I was a specialist but I didn't, and couldn't be expected to, know everything. I saw that I needed the support of my colleagues, that there was much I could learn from them and that sharing ideas and concerns works to everyone's benefit. It also became uncomfortably clear to me that I'd wanted others to look up to me. It's great for your self-esteem and self-image when patients or students hang on to your every word.

I began to learn from my students as well – some of them have placements in environments that I'm not familiar with and their feedback enhanced my practice. I found that the relationship I had with them changed, for the good I might add. It became more open, more comfortable for me and for them I think, and more relaxed. We could have a joke together – unthinkable in the early days. This shift provided opportunities for me to support them in new ways. I remember, for example, the first time one of my students confided to me her terror when forced to use a computer. I was able to point her in the direction of someone who could give her some extra help and she was happier and more focused afterwards. In the earlier days of teaching I doubt I'd have even noticed her discomfort.

I also became involved in the marketing and promotion of new courses. It wasn't something I was keen to do as I didn't see myself as a natural salesperson, but it was dumped on me by my line manager and at first I just got on with it but now I actually enjoy this aspect of my work. I probably see myself as a jack of all trades now: acupuncturist, teacher, colleague, counsellor, salesperson. But I'm also more adaptable, more able to respond to people and situations in a professional way.

It's not all plain sailing though. When I first began teaching I saw myself first and foremost as an acupuncturist who teaches, but the teaching side of my profession soon took on a more central role. Acupuncture and Chinese medicine do have a huge practical element but there is a lot of theory to go with it, and I spend an increasing proportion of my professional life in a classroom. I really enjoy teaching but it leaves very little opportunity to treat patients myself, and this is the problem – what credibility do I have with students if I don't actually do the job myself? I haven't yet resolved this one.

Critical thinking activity

» How did Jay's professional identity inform his relationships with colleagues and learners when he first became a teacher?

» How did his professional identity change over time?

» *What conflicts does Jay have within his professional identity?*

Jay saw himself as a professional acupuncturist who knew best. The status that came with being the expert enhanced his self-image but his attitude isolated him from learners and colleagues. His professional identity changed over time in a number of ways, from sole expert to collegiate, from subject specialist to teacher. He also embraced a pastoral role and was required to take on a marketing role.

You can see from Jay's story that professional identity is based on professional expertise in both pedagogy and subject specialism and provides a framework for how teachers should act. Sometimes there is choice within this framework as Jay discovered when he took on a more collegiate approach and a pastoral role. At other times it is imposed on you, as happened when Jay was required to involve himself in marketing and promoting new courses. Jay's story also shows how professional identity evolves through professional experience and is modified by others: colleagues, managers and learners. For Jay this shift in identity allowed him to have the open, honest and trusting relationships with colleagues and learners that enhance professional practice.

There is conflict between Jay's professional identity as an acupuncturist and as a teacher. He says that his credibility with students is undermined because he no longer does the job that he trains others to do. Dual professionalism can even lead to a sort of professional identity crisis. Are you a computer specialist who teaches, or a teacher who used to be a computer specialist? If you are promoted into college management, are you a manager who used to be a teacher and in turn used to be a computer specialist?

Critical thinking activity: professional identity – changes and conflicts

» *How do you see your professional identity and how does it inform your practice? How has it been modified through your experience? What aspects of it have been imposed on you?*

» *Wenger (1998, p 151) urges teachers to 'position themselves mainly within the teaching community rather than in their vocational area'. Do you agree? What conflicts, if any, do you see between your identity as a subject specialist who teaches and a teacher with a subject specialism?*

Self-image and self-esteem

Jay's self-image was enhanced through the status that came with being the font of all knowledge. He is not alone. We know through the work of psychologists that we thrive on the high esteem we experience when others look up to us. In fact, self-esteem is so important to us that we are programmed to actively search for it. Mark Leary, a leading researcher on self-consciousness suggests that we are constantly on the lookout for signs that we are valued, or not, by those around us, a process which he says takes place largely unconsciously (Leary, cited in Haidt, 2012). When we detect positive signals our esteem level rises; when these signals are absent or we detect negative signals it drops. If it plummets too far our fears and thoughts of failure surface and we may begin to question our abilities. The psychologist

Denis Lawrence (1996) suggests that the higher our self-esteem the more confident and the more motivated we are. When we like ourselves and are proud of our achievements we are more likely to like others; when we value ourselves we are more able to relate to learners and colleagues alike with warmth and enthusiasm.

Yet the majority of us find it quite difficult to even identify our talents and skills, let alone to celebrate them, to give ourselves a pat on the back for the things we can do and for the qualities we possess. We find it much easier to see our failures and shortcomings. Teachers are no different and can often find it difficult to acknowledge, even to themselves, that they are good at what they do. Yet it's highly unlikely that they would be in the teaching profession, and they certainly wouldn't want to stay for too long unless they had an abundance of qualities and talents.

Critical thinking activity: what are you worth?

» *Make an inventory of as many of your talents, skills, achievements, accomplishments and personal qualities as you can think of. You may initially struggle to think of many. Don't be put off. You will find lists of skills and personal qualities online (there are a couple of helpful sites at the end of the chapter). You may also find it hard to give yourself credit where it is due but you don't need to be an expert in order to credit yourself with a particular skill or quality. You may also wish to ask those who know you well to help. Your inventory will be substantial and you may well be surprised at its depth and breadth.*

Values

The IfL Code of Professional Practice (Appendix B) is exactly that, a code of *practice* or behaviour. It lists a number of values but describes in detail what constitutes expected professional behaviour for each value. In contrast, the LLUK standards place the emphasis firmly on professional values rather than on behaviour or action; professional values are thus understood in terms of what is required of teachers, who should value, for example, learning and learners. One possible explanation for this approach could lie in the definition of the word *value* as 'a principle or standard of behaviour'. In other words our values guide our actions, so with this in mind it does make sense to focus on professional values: if these are on the right lines the hope is that the right action will follow.

Personal values

With professional values as a guide is it necessary to look at personal values? The answer must be yes, because you can say without a shadow of doubt that in teaching it is not possible to switch off personal values. The expectation is that your personal values are pretty much along the same lines as the professional values but there is a difficulty here concerning the differences between the two. Personal values differ from professional values in two ways. Firstly, whereas professional values are visible – you can find them, for example, in the LLUK standards – personal values are implicit, not necessarily acknowledged. This means that you are often unaware of many of the values you hold. Secondly, whereas professional values are shared with colleagues and others, personal values are just that, personal, individual. This means that our individual values won't necessarily be the same as the next person's, although, oddly, we can be quite fazed when we discover this to be the case. One good example is if you become rattled when someone queue jumps. Implicitly you value the fairness of taking turns and expect others to value it too. Inevitably in teaching, your colleagues and learners will have different values from the ones you hold, and how you manage this difference will inform your professional practice.

Here is one teacher's experience of trying to manage the gap between her personal values and those of her colleagues.

CASE STUDY

Mel's values

Mel is a catering lecturer at a large FE college where she has a very busy and demanding timetable. She is trying her best to do a professional job but it seems some of her values are out of kilter with a minority of people around her and it's making things difficult for her. She is talking to Jo, a friend and colleague, over a cup of coffee after work.

I've had a bit of an up and down day. First thing this morning I was faced with my first-year Front-of-House students who should be well into their project reports by now. Yet half of them were saying they didn't know what they were supposed to do as they hadn't done report writing yet in their functional skills classes. Steph, the functional skills lecturer should have covered it by now, it's her job not mine. We don't get on too well and I'm wondering whether she's just being awkward. If I have to allocate time to teach them how to write sentences I won't have time to do what I'm here to do – teach them catering skills. So I decided that I wasn't going to waste valuable time going through the report writing with those who hadn't yet made a start. I'd already planned some much-needed revision for this morning so that's what we did.

Then we had a meeting later on to discuss the stand we are having at the spring fair. There were six of us but two of the others hadn't prepared anything so had nothing to contribute and another arrived half an hour late and hadn't even bothered to read the info sheet that I'd e-mailed. I bet they just couldn't be bothered. And of course, this meant that those of us who had bothered had to shoulder the bulk of the planning.

Critical thinking activity

» What are the personal values that Mel holds that appear to be out of kilter with some of the people around her? How have they helped to form her attitude to her colleagues? What judgements has she made based on her values?

» What LLUK professional values do you think are undermined in the situation that Mel has described regarding the writing of project reports? Is Mel correct when, *talking about who is responsible for the report writing, she says, 'It's her job not mine'? Give reasons.*

»   *In practical terms is there anything that Mel can do to improve the situation with regard to the project reports and the team meeting?*

You probably sympathise with Mel. Perhaps you've even had some similar experiences. Clearly, she values fairness, punctuality and being organised and should certainly be applauded for her commitment to high levels of professionalism. But Mel has assumed that Steph has probably not done the report writing on purpose just to be awkward. This is possible but unlikely, and Mel has no valid reason to believe this to be the case. Mel judges some of her colleagues at the meeting as lazy, again without justification.

Two of the LLUK professional values, 'Learners, their progress and development' (Domain A AS1) and 'Collaboration with other individuals' (Domain A AS5) are now undermined. Mel believes that the responsibility for the project writing rests firmly in Steph's lap, yet there is a requirement for all teachers, whatever their subject specialism, to support their learners in developing their literacy skills. Instead of going over the project writing with her learners there and then she decided instead to continue with the revision she'd planned. This decision might put some of her learners behind with their work.

Practical measures to improve each of these situations require some form of dialogue. The form that dialogue might take will be covered later in this chapter.

Would it be a good idea for Mel to reassess her values, perhaps put less emphasis on good time keeping and being organised? Perhaps, but this is much easier said than done because, as you have just seen, personal values are implicit, unacknowledged. The chances are that Mel doesn't even realise she holds these values. How easy would it be for her to change something she is not aware of?

Critical thinking activity: identifying personal values in practice

»   *Can you think of a situation where your values have differed from those of someone you know, for example, a colleague, a family member, a friend or a learner? How did this affect your attitude to them?*

»   *The FE sector is now free to develop its own standards of professional values. How do you feel these changes will affect your professional practice?*

Virtues

If Mel is unaware of her values she might well be stuck in this unfortunate scenario, but there are possible solutions. One tool at her disposal to help solve the problem would be for her to think about virtues rather than values. Virtues are character traits that have a morally good or desirable element, for example, kindness or loyalty. We hear very little about them these days; they are out of date, banished along with chivalry and honour to the realm of knights in shining amour, rescuing maidens in distress. In fact, moral debate itself is almost always in terms of right behaviour or right action rather than the character traits of the individual. For example, you might debate whether euthanasia is a morally right action, but you would be unlikely to be involved in a debate about the merits of, say, integrity or perseverance. Yet this hasn't always been the case. In many societies throughout history virtues have played a greater role in daily life.

Virtues have a distinct advantage over values. They are more visible and substantial and therefore easier to get a handle on. In fact, the philosopher Socrates likened virtues to skills such as woodwork or medicine. This analogy seems odd at first but it does make sense because virtues do have a number of things in common with skills. They are both acquired, they are both admired and valued by others and they are both beneficial to have (Kenny, 2010). These similarities between skills and virtues alone seem reason enough to take virtues seriously but there is another reason why they are well worth considering. The original Greek word for virtue, αρετή was understood to mean excellence. Now this interpretation would appear to be very much at the heart of the concept of what it means to be professional.

Suppose Mel were to decide that life would be a little easier if she were able to develop the virtue of flexibility. However, Kenny does point out a small fly in the ointment. There is one major difference between skills and virtues. If you want to develop a skill, for example in woodwork or medicine, you go to an expert carpenter or doctor. Yet when it comes to developing a virtue, where do you find an expert? You are in fact left to your own devices here but oddly, a do-it-yourself approach may well be the best approach, especially in terms of the old adage, 'practice makes perfect'. And as far as the eighteenth-century German philosopher Immanuel Kant was concerned, virtues, just like skills, are acquired by practice and lost by disuse – in other words we develop a virtue by copying it and using it: 'For when men play these roles virtues are gradually established whose appearance had up until now only been affected' (Kant, cited in Comte-Sponville, 2003, p 12). And indeed, this is just what one polymath, the American statesman Benjamin Franklin did. He compiled a list of the virtues he wanted to develop and concentrated on one or two each week, keeping a detailed record of how he was doing. While this dedication to self-improvement may not be to everyone's taste the idea of developing a few useful virtues is certainly worth considering.

There are several writers whom you may find helpful in identifying some of these useful virtues. Arthur, Davison and Lewis, for example, ask the reader to consider the practice of a number of virtues in teaching including

> *dignity, integrity, diligence, loyalty, honour, truth, courtesy, love, fairness, moderation, caring, compassion, sensitivity, justice, tolerance, kindness, responsibility, respect, enthusiasm, flexibility, reliability, tact, confidentiality.*
>
> (Arthur, Davison and Lewis, 2005, p 29)

In recent years there has also been renewed interest in virtues within a branch of psychology called 'Positive Psychology' and a classification of the virtues that are widely endorsed across societies. Some of the virtues included in that classification are:

• 	wisdom: curiosity, judgement, ingenuity, emotional intelligence;

- courage: valor, perseverance, integrity;
- temperance: self-control, prudence, humility.

(Seligman, 2004)

The point of the classification is that it provides an opportunity to consider and debate the role virtues might have in professional life. It's possible to take any virtue and identify it in professional practice. For example, you can take the virtue 'patience' and recall occasions you have been patient. You can ask yourself whether you are patient with learners and colleagues, whether you find it easy or difficult to be patient and in what situations? You can do the same with 'reliability' and think of concrete examples of your reliability. You can ask yourself if you are always reliable, most of the time or less often? And you can do the same with any virtue.

Critical thinking activity: identifying virtues in practice

» *Choose from the above virtues those you think are desirable in a teacher and give reasons for your choice.*

» *For each of the virtues you have chosen, identify it in your professional practice as described above and suggest opportunities where you could develop it further.*

You might also wish to visit Seligman's website (www.authentichappiness.org) and complete an online assessment of your personal virtues. If, having done the above critical learning activity and/or visited the website, you find a number of virtues that you want to develop, remember to think of them as Socrates and Kant did, as skills that can be perfected through use and lost through disuse, although perhaps not with the same dedication and enthusiasm as Benjamin Franklin. And there is reward in discovering the many occasions where you can feel particularly *virtuous*. And this is the point of course. There are no right or wrong answers. However, in *The Ethical Teacher*, Elizabeth Campbell points out that there has to be, within teaching, a shared ethical core.

> *There is no one uniform or generic model of the ethical teacher who comes in many forms reflective of the uniqueness of individuals. However ethical teachers do share a similar sense of moral agency and purpose framed by a deep regard for core moral and ethical principles such as... justice, kindness, honesty and respect for others.*

(Campbell, 2003, p 140)

Emotions

One of the virtues mentioned above, emotional intelligence, seen also as a skill and therefore sometimes referred to as emotional literacy, warrants some further exploration. The Oxford Dictionary defines emotional intelligence as 'the capacity to be aware of, control and express one's emotions and to handle interpersonal relationships judiciously and empathetically'. The term was first coined around forty years ago and was made popular by a number of publications in the 1980s and 1990s, including one by Daniel Goleman entitled *Working with Emotional Intelligence* (1999), but the concept on which it is based is far from new, being rooted in Buddhism, Confucianism and in much Western philosophy. To see how emotional literacy might be relevant to professional practice, take another look at Mel. She has been describing her day to Jo, her colleague. Now she carries on with the story.

CASE STUDY

Mel's feelings

As far as the project writing was concerned I decided the best approach was to get my line manager to sort things out with Steph. She needs to be told that I'm not prepared to do her work.

I managed to sort out the fiasco of the team meeting. Once we had finished with the planning issues I had a word with the three who hadn't prepared for the meeting and had therefore been next to useless. I was very assertive and clear. I told them that it was unprofessional and not fair on the rest of us to turn up at a meeting and not bother to do any preparation for it. To be honest, I felt I was banging my head against a brick wall. I try to do a professional job but sometimes it seems like I am the only one who's bothered.

By this time I was ready for a coffee and a bun. I also managed to grab a few minutes to phone home to find out if Toby, my dog, was feeling any better. He's getting on a bit and I've been worried about him as he's been poorly the last couple of days. It was good news and things got a whole lot better after that.

My afternoon was with my group of advanced hospitality students and there was a real buzz to the session. On Saturday two of the teaching staff are getting married and the reception is going to be held in the training restaurant with the students doing everything themselves. For many of them it will be their first professional engagement and we are all excited. They are working very hard to make sure it's a perfect day. At the end of the session they didn't want to go home so we did an impromptu dress rehearsal that involved a lot of clapping and cheering. For me this is what it's all about – this is why I'm a teacher.

Critical thinking activity

» *What range of emotions do you think Mel experienced that may have influenced her responses to the events of the day?*

» *How do you think Mel's response to her colleagues at the team meeting would have made them feel?*

» *How might you have dealt with these issues?*

The chances are that Mel began the day feeling anxious about Toby, her cherished dog. As for the issue of the project writing she probably felt irritated with Steph and frustrated that she couldn't get on with what she'd originally planned to do. But she may well have felt apprehensive about challenging Steph as they didn't get on so she opted instead to pass this responsibility on to her line manager. Long term this problem does need sorting, and the professional approach would be to speak to Steph herself and try to come to some agreement that they are both happy with. As for her colleagues at the team meeting it is likely that feelings of resentment were at the heart of her response. The afternoon session with her hospitality learners gave Mel an opportunity to experience and share with her learners some of the positive emotions that are vital for professional practice: enthusiasm, interest, pleasure, humour, excitement and so on.

Mel's negative criticism of her colleagues after the team meeting is likely to have left them feeling chastised and possibly resentful. A professional approach would have been one which stressed the importance and value of their contributions to the team, one aimed at leaving them feeling keen to do more work for future meetings.

We like to think of ourselves as rational, reasoning human beings. In reality though, like Mel, at times we all behave in ways that are anything but rational and reasonable. Rather than reason, it is our emotions that often drive our behaviour, a fact that has been pointed out to us throughout history by a host of philosophers, some of whom see our very existence as a constant battle between our reasoning selves and our emotional selves. In *Metamorphoses* the Roman poet Ovid provides a vivid image of his battle between reason and the emotion of desire when he confesses, 'Desire and reason are pulling in different directions. I see the right way and approve it but follow the wrong'. It's easy here to picture Ovid at the open biscuit barrel with his hand poised over the fig biscuits!

Some contemporary theorists believe that our emotions 'play a fundamental role in our ability to function at all' (Gilbert, 2009, p 26). There is good reason for this view. Our emotions go back millions of years. We've had a long time to get used to expressing them so we use them automatically, effortlessly and instinctively. Our ability to reason, on the other hand, when compared to emotions, is a fairly new addition, less than a couple of million years (Haidt, 2012). We've had less time to get used to reason so it doesn't kick in quite so easily and effortlessly. It takes time – we have to stop and think, to reason things out.

It is inevitable in teaching that your emotions are engaged with learners and with colleagues. Indeed your emotions play an important and valuable role in teaching. Your feelings of interest, empathy and enthusiasm, for example, enable you to inspire, to support and encourage learners. But situations can arise in teaching where it's all too easy to feel irritated, frustrated and angry. How do you respond to them? The best response, of course, is to stop and allow reason to kick in, but in practice the temptation is to express irritations, frustrations and so on to whoever we believe is responsible for making us feel the way we do. We can express these feelings as nagging, complaining, sarcasm, negative criticism or even losing our temper. However, we express the majority of feelings through body language, especially through facial expression, so negative emotions will be evident in the frown, the grimace, the look to heaven, the shrug of the shoulders, the long weary sigh and so on. These responses are seldom, if ever, welcomed by the recipient or helpful in finding solutions and sustaining professional relationships.

Critical thinking activity: identifying emotional responses in practice

» *Identify an occasion when a positive emotion such as interest or pleasure informed your response. How do you think your response affected the other person or persons involved?*

» *Do the same with a negative emotion such as anger or anxiety. How might you have responded using reason rather than emotion?*

A major aspect of developing emotional literacy is gaining an awareness of how your emotions affect your interactions with others. With colleagues and learners alike professionalism is about taking responsibility for emotions. It's about searching for strategies that will produce positive outcomes in relationships. This means recognising and celebrating those emotions that enhance your teaching relationships, and managing those that can be detrimental. Philosophers ancient and modern believe the best way to do this is by stopping and giving the reasoning self a chance to work things out.

A second aspect of emotional literacy, equally important in teaching, is the capacity to relate to others with empathy; this aspect is covered in a later chapter.

Critical thinking activity: research emotional literacy

» *Use internet and library sources to find out more about emotional literacy.*

Beliefs

Everyone has a set of personal beliefs about the world and their place in it, what is important to them and how things should be. For example, you might believe that there should be a more equal distribution of wealth throughout the world. Your belief system, your philosophy of life, will be based on your values, your background, what you've learned and your life experience. Within this belief system are your beliefs about education, for example, its nature and purpose. You may not have articulated or even acknowledged these beliefs but nevertheless, they inform your approach to teaching and guide you in your relationships with learners and colleagues.

So what is your personal philosophy of education? To get you thinking, here are some statements that illustrate some very different educational philosophies. Read them through and then answer the questions below.

1. One of the aims of education is to encourage learners to become mature, moral and responsible people. The teacher's job is to provide an arena where learners can discover for themselves. Education is more than imparting facts or getting qualifications. It should be a place where learners can flourish, where they can work together, to co-operate, gain skills and knowledge and build confidence and self-esteem.

2.   Learner-centred sounds great in principle and 'filling empty pitchers' went out of fashion a long time ago, but at the end of the day there's so much they need to know and often the 'sage-on-the-stage' approach is the most effective.

3.   You can't argue with the fact that some people are never going to be brain surgeons. What you have to do is give them the best support for whatever their role in life is going to be. It needs to be practical, relevant to society, aimed at meeting each individual learner's needs and supporting them in fulfilling their potential and achieving their aspirations.

4.   What's the point of producing people qualified to do this or that if they can't get the job that they have spent years working for? In many ways education is no different from any other product, supplying what the economy requires.

Critical thinking activity: identifying your philosophy of education

»   *What beliefs are implicit in each of these statements?*

»   *What is your opinion of each statement? Why do you agree or disagree with it?*

All these statements raise as many questions as they answer. With regard to the first statement, no one could argue with the worthy aims of learners flourishing, co-operating, gaining confidence and self-esteem. But is the teacher's role to enhance self-esteem or to stretch and challenge learners? These two may not be compatible anyway (Ecclestone et al., cited in Tummons, 2008, p 29). In the second statement, if teaching is about imparting facts, this raises the question of who decides which facts are imparted. You? Awarding bodies (Wallace, 2007, p 72)? In the third statement, if education means meeting the needs of society, does this mean that the purpose of education is, 'to train people to take up their proper roles' (Scrimshaw, 1980, cited in Armitage et al., 2007, p 192)? This then raises questions of how and by whom that role is decided (Wallace, 2007). You may not agree with the final statement's description of education as a product and teaching a response to the needs of the economy. Yet many of the programmes run in colleges, in service industry and elsewhere are skills for work programmes.

It is clear from even such a cursory look at these different ideas that philosophies of teaching and learning are complex and often contradictory. There are no easy answers; on the contrary there will always be more questions. A number of great thinkers have written about their philosophy of education, much of which has provided the framework for current approaches to teaching and learning. Most generic teaching books have a section on the philosophy of education. *Teaching and Training in Post-Compulsory Education*, by Armitage et al. (2007), for example, has an informative but concise section on the educational philosophies of Socrates, Rousseau and John Dewey.

Critical thinking activity: research philosophies of education

»   *Research the philosophy of three educational thinkers. You might select three who have been cited in this chapter, or find others of your own. Choose the one that is most in sympathy with your own philosophical beliefs about education. Record the main points of the philosophy you have chosen and the reasons for your choice.*

Conclusion

Many teachers felt that the LLUK standards were imposed from above on people already doing a professional job, but they can provide a framework to guide practice. This shift from imposition to guidance makes it even more important for teachers to take responsibility for their own professionalism, to look inward to discover how their identity and self-image, their personal values, emotions and beliefs inform their professional practice. This means that you now need to be more self-aware, to enable you to respond wisely and professionally in a whole raft of teaching situations.

Chapter reflections

» *Professional identity is a process mediated by your experience and your relationships with colleagues, learners and others.*

» *Your values, beliefs and emotions inform both your teaching and your professional relationships.*

» *Identifying and using virtues can enhance your professional practice.*

Taking it further

Comte-Sponville, A (2003) *A Short Treatise on the Great Virtues*. London: Vintage.
This contemporary French philosopher shows how a range of virtues can be useful in everyday life.

Haidt, J (2012) *The Righteous Mind*. London: Penguin.
In this very accessible book the American psychologist Jonathan Haidt provides a wealth of evidence to show why we hold the beliefs we do and why others sometimes disagree with us.

References

Armitage, A, Bryant, R, Dunnill, R, Flanagan, K, Hayes, D, Hudson, A, Kent, J, Lawes, S and Renwick, M (2007) *Teaching and Training in Post-Compulsory Education*. Maidenhead: McGraw Hill.
Arthur, J, Davison, J and Lewis, M (2005) *Professional Values and Practice*. Abingdon: Routledge.
Campbell, E (2003) *The Ethical Teacher*. Maidenhead: OU Press.
Comte-Sponville, A (2003) *A Short Treatise on the Great Virtues*. London: Vintage.
Gilbert, P (2009) *The Compassionate Mind*. London: Constable.
Goleman, D (1999) *Working with Emotional Intelligence*. London: Bloomsbury.
Haidt, J (2012) *The Righteous Mind*. London: Penguin.
Kenny, A (2010) *The New History of Western Philosophy*. Oxford: OUP.
Lawrence, D (1996) *Enhancing Self-Esteem in the Classroom*. London: Paul Chapman Publishing Ltd.
Sachs, J (2011) *The Activist Teaching Profession*. Maidenhead: OU Press.
Seligman, M (2004) *Authentic Happiness*. London: Simon & Schuster.
Tummons, J (2008) *Becoming a Professional Tutor in the Lifelong Learning Sector*. Exeter: Learning Matters.

Wallace, S (2007) *Teaching, Tutoring and Training in the Lifelong Learning Sector*. Exeter: Learning Matters.

Wenger, E (1998) *Communities of Practice: Learning, Meaning and Identity*. Cambridge: Cambridge University Press.

Websites

www.authentichappiness.org (last accessed 6 February 2014)

www.ifl.ac.uk (last accessed 6 February 2014)

www.gurusoftware.com (last accessed 6 February 2014)

www.sc.edu/career/pdf/identity (last accessed 6 February 2014)

4 Curiosity enlightened the cat: looking beyond 'learner'

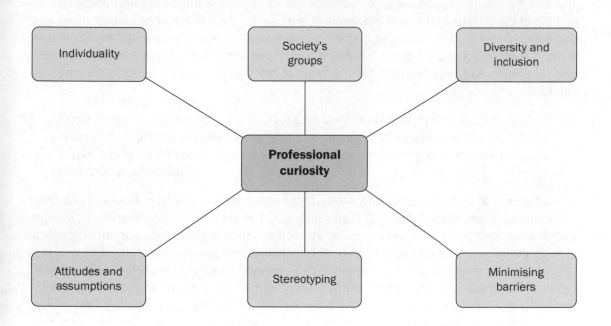

Chapter aims

This chapter will help you to:

- identify ways to support all learners;
- recognise and respond to the diversity of your learners;
- promote inclusion;
- assess your beliefs and assumptions about your learners.

Introduction

The central theme of the previous chapter was the character of the teacher; the focus now shifts to the relationship between teacher and learner. As a professional teacher you will want to establish relationships with your learners that best support them in their learning.

The chapter begins by focusing on each learner as a unique individual and continues by looking at the different groups, for example by age, social class or ethnicity that your learners belong to. A key feature throughout is your professional curiosity. Hopefully this is evident in your subject specialism but it would be a mistake to think that this is where it might end. Teachers, suggests Jeanne Hitching, need to tap into the natural curiosity they had as children:

> *Actively engage your professional curiosity again... Children often go through a stage when their curiosity about life is apparent. As we grow older we tend to lose the skill of asking meaningful questions. You need to redevelop your professional curiosity.*
>
> (Hitching, 2008, p 9)

The emphasis in this chapter is on your curiosity about your learners, curiosity about their experiences, their motivations and their concerns. The chapter seeks to show how what you discover can better equip you to support each of your learners. They are undoubtedly a diverse group, and a good starting point is to consider the nature of this diversity and the implications for your professional relationships with them. Valuing diversity is fundamental to professional practice. Commitment to it is evident in the Lifelong Learning UK (LLUK, 2007) professional standards, and it permeates throughout all six domains. Teachers are called upon to value and celebrate it through professional relationships with their learners, and much has been written on how this can be achieved. Ashmore et al. (2010), for example, stress the responsibility of teachers to create an inclusive learning environment that enables all learners to maximise their potential.

So far, so good, but how might valuing diversity be achieved in practical terms? The intention in this chapter is to answer that question by providing practical illustrations of what teachers can achieve through their professional relationships with their learners.

The theme of curiosity is continued through the chapter with the concluding section focusing on your curiosity about your own attitudes to your learners; and again much has been written on this issue. For example, Baker and Blair (2008) point out that teachers need to be aware of their own sentiments in relation to the wide range of diversity they are likely to encounter in their learners. Thus, this final section shows how curiosity about your own beliefs and a willingness to examine them can lead you to greater understanding and celebration of diversity.

The learner as an individual

The concept of diversity encompasses acceptance and respect. It means understanding that each individual is unique.

(University of Oregon, diversity policy statement)

At the completion of a learning programme learners are often asked to complete a course evaluation; this provides important feedback on their experiences of learning. Often these evaluations require only tick box answers but sometimes there is space to give more detailed feedback on the experience of learning. When this is the case one thing that often strikes you on reading through these evaluations is the diversity of the learners' responses. This is hardly surprising as each learner's perception of their learning experience will be unique, based to a large extent on their background, life experience and so on. This seems glaringly obvious but even with a learner-centred philosophy it's easy to lose sight of this fact. The label 'learner' itself can be a barrier. Of course they are learners, at least for that period of time, be it two hours once a week or much longer, just as for that period of time you are the teacher. But at the end of the session or the end of the day, teachers and learners alike walk out of one life and into another.

What do you know about Steve or Suzie? Perhaps Steve and Suzie have spoken a little about themselves at some time during a class session. Even so it is easy to see them as learners and less easy to look beyond the label. So what's the point of looking beyond 'learner'? It is after all why Steve and Suzie are there – to be learners. How does seeing each learner as an individual enhance professional practice?

It is worthwhile here to consider an experienced teacher, one who has a professional approach to his teaching, who takes pride in supporting each and every one of his learners and who believes that what he knows about each of them helps him to do this more effectively. Read through the following case study and answer the questions that follow.

CASE STUDY

Joseph's end-of-course evaluations

Joseph works for a training agency that specialises in providing a range of business courses to local small- and medium-sized businesses. His learners are diverse: different social and ethnic backgrounds, a variety of professions and a wide age range. Many of Joseph's learners would have been sent on his courses as a result of restructure within their organisation, and consequently some are less enthusiastic than others about attending. His learners have just completed a Business Improvements Techniques course and are giving feedback on their thoughts and feelings about their experience of learning. Here they are talking about some of the things that have enabled them to learn and to enjoy their learning.

Grace

I really needed this qualification as I was in line for promotion at work. Joseph seemed to cotton on to how important it was for me. I didn't ask him to but he offered me some references for extra reading if I was interested. The other thing that was helpful for me in particular was how relevant the majority of the activities and discussions we had were to the reality of my experience within the organisation I work for. I think the others felt the same – there was a lot of scope to feed off each other's ideas and experiences.

Tony

I suspect it was pretty obvious on day one that I thought it was a bit of a waste of time for me to do this course as I'm due to retire soon. But in the introduction at the start we were all asked to say a bit about ourselves and would you believe it, at the tea break Joseph buttonholed me and asked me the best local place for fishing – well you can't argue with a fellow angler can you?

Millie

I'm not all that outgoing and can feel a bit anxious with lots of other people but in the first two or three sessions I found I was always put in a small group for any group work. This made it much easier for me to join in all the activities and soon I was really enjoying it. I knew I would find it extremely stressful if I was asked to do a presentation to the class but Joseph never made me feel awkward about not doing it. On the other hand I am really good with written work and he gave me lots of opportunities to record our group discussions and activities so I always felt part of the team.

Oliver

Joseph speaks pretty clearly anyway, but he seemed to know I had a problem with my hearing and without making a thing of it, whenever he spoke to me he always looked directly at me.

Hua

We were about to start the Health and Safety session of the course and Joseph must have remembered that I said I have experience in this field and he asked me if I would be interested in giving a short talk to the rest of the group. I was, and I did and it was great, although the others certainly put me through my paces with their questions at the end. And you know, I think doing it helped all of us take the new stuff on board much better.

Neil

There was no way that I was going to change my view about being in a classroom. I never liked school and I knew I wasn't going to like this experience. I was only there because I wasn't given a choice. And I haven't changed my view – I won't go on another course unless I'm made to. Having said that, if I was forced to do another one I hope I'd get someone like Joseph. We had this unspoken agreement – I put in some effort and join in and he would be OK about me needing an extra five minutes at tea break to go out for a smoke. He drew the line at ten minutes but it was worth a try.

Critical thinking activity

» *Joseph appeared to know quite a lot about his learners. How might he have gained this knowledge and how did it inform his practice? Do you agree with his decision to allow Neil an extra five minutes' coffee break? Give reasons.*

» *What else might teachers want to be curious about when listening to and observing their learners?*

Joseph would have been considering a number of questions relating to each of his learners. Why are they here? Did they choose to come and, if so, why this subject? What are their expectations? What do they want from their learning? What do they already know about the subject? What is their previous experience of education? How confident do they feel? What support might they need? He would have made a point of listening to his learners and observing their body language, recognising that each would have individual feelings about being there, individual needs to be met and a unique contribution to make. What he learned about each of them informed his responses.

Grace may have spoken about her need for good grades but even if she hadn't Joseph would have been aware of her enthusiasm and her desire to take on more work. He would have been on the lookout for learners who needed to be stretched just as much as those who would need extra support. During the initial introduction to the course it is likely that Tony would have voiced his reservations about attending and Joseph would have observed Tony's apathetic demeanour, the resigned expression and slumping back in the chair. Joseph used the knowledge of their shared interest in angling to engage with Tony in order to give him at least one reason to be there.

It is likely that Joseph would have been aware of Millie's anxiety from the start. Again, the signs would have been in her body language, her reluctance perhaps to make eye contact with him or with other learners and/or to speak. Just think for a moment how difficult it must be for someone like Millie to attend a programme that she would have known would give her so much anxiety. This takes considerable courage because communication skills, along with many literacy skills, are visible to everyone. This means that any failure is a public failure. Millie is far from alone in feeling anxious, and learners' anxieties are not only to do with communicating. As to the causes and nature of their anxiety Jenny Rogers (2001) suggests that the major factors are fear of being out of their depth, of being shown up, of being put on the spot, and/or negative memories of school. Rogers believes it is best to assume that most adult learners are anxious as they approach their learning, even many who appear to be confident.

Professionalism can often lie in small things that teachers do or that they don't do. Oliver's comments are a good example of two small things, one that Joseph did and one that he didn't do. Each made a difference to Oliver's experience. Firstly, Joseph looked at Oliver when he spoke to him and secondly, in Oliver's words 'he didn't make a thing of it'. This second point is important. Here is a scenario for you to consider. You have lost the sight in one of your eyes. You have adapted but you know that when you are going to be sitting with a group of people (as, for example, in a classroom) you need to ensure that your seat is one which will give you a view that takes in as many of your fellow learners as possible. You don't want to say anything about your restricted vision; you want to appear to be the same as everyone else. Assuming the teacher knows about your disability, perhaps they can find a way, without making it too obvious to the rest of the class, to earmark a seat for you in the first session or two until everyone has become used to sitting in a certain chair. The point here is that a big difference can be made to a learner's experience when teachers notice small things. Disability comes in many guises. In addition to physical disability you may also encounter learners with learning difficulties, mental health problems, dyslexia or autistic spectrum disorder.

Joseph had learned that Hua had some experience with Health and Safety issues. Asking her to give a short talk about her work showed that he saw her as an individual and valued her knowledge and experience. Individual learners have a wealth of knowledge and experience that is unique to them. What they have to offer could be in their experience, their background, specific knowledge or a particular talent or skill, and much of it can be harnessed in very practical ways, through formal presentations, impromptu talks, demonstrations, providing background information and so on.

Neil was a learner with the potential to disrupt. Like Tony he had been made to attend, but unlike Tony, who was apathetic, Neil felt resentful. He'd never liked school and didn't want to be in a classroom. Even if Joseph knew nothing about Neil's previous experience of education he would have been aware of his feelings at finding himself in a place he didn't want to be. Joseph finds a way to give something of value to Neil – an extra five minutes at the end of the coffee breaks. For Neil this is recognition of his unhappy feelings about having to attend. Adult learners enter education with unique histories and experiences that would have informed their values and their attitudes to learning. It is hoped that the majority of learners have a positive attitude; they want to be there, are motivated and enthusiastic. Inevitably, a small minority of learners will have a negative attitude, either because of failure at school or through the influence of those around such as family, colleagues and friends. These learners may see little value in education and little reason to be where they are. The challenge for a professional teacher is to work towards changing this negative attitude into a more positive approach to learning.

You could say that teaching has a lot in common with gardening. You are likely to come into gardening as a novice and are faced with a range of plants you know nothing about. You research the theory, read the gardening books and get to work. Most of the plants in your garden do pretty well, some do exceptionally well; they flourish despite your mistakes. Some are really tricky. No matter what you do, they struggle. But over time you gain experience and importantly, you get to know your garden and your plants. You get to know that each plant is unique. No matter that it is planted in the same soil as its neighbour, it grows at its own pace and develops in its own way and you have to recognise and meet its individual needs. Professional gardeners, and here I mean gardeners who love gardening, who take pride in it and get a kick when their plants flourish, are great observers. They are curious. They take notice. They take the time to see that this plant isn't getting quite enough of something it needs or that the plant has a problem, perhaps it is being nibbled by a miniscule pest.

At the risk of conjuring up in your mind images of learners plagued by greenfly, I think it takes little effort to transfer this analogy into a teaching context. Joseph didn't see his learners only in their learning role. He looked beyond learner. He was curious. He took notice and saw individuals who had unique needs, experiences and contributions.

Critical thinking activity: curiosity in practice

» *Choose one of your learners and write down what you know about them. Does any of the information you have recorded about them better enable you to support them and, if so, in what way? (You may wish to repeat this with other learners.)*

The learner as a group member

The starting point is to use the term diversity to describe different kinds of people working or studying in the organisation. Most often it is used to designate 'others' as different from themselves. Thus the term is frequently used to categorise individuals in terms of visible difference.

(Lumby et al. cited in Ashmore et al., 2010, p 59)

So far the emphasis has been on seeing each learner as an individual with specific needs and a unique experience. However, professional teachers will recognise that each individual is also a group member and will wish to learn about the groups they belong to in order to respond appropriately. They will, for example, wish to be sensitive to a learner's religious or ethnic affiliations. In exploring how this can best be achieved it is worthwhile returning to Joseph, that paragon of virtue, and continuing with the feedback from his learners.

CASE STUDY

More from Joseph's end-of-course evaluations

Tony

I wasn't the only one on the course who was nearing retirement. There were three of us. We had a laugh about it on the first morning, called ourselves the three old codgers, but to be honest all three of us felt a bit embarrassed, sensing that the younger ones wouldn't be in the slightest bit interested in anything us oldies had to say. We thought we might look stupid, say the wrong thing or have a senior moment and not be able to think of the answer to a question. In fact the opposite happened. Joseph kept on getting us to give our opinions so the others could see things from a broader point of view. And it was interesting because often we were able to offer a new way of looking at things simply because we were older.

Neil

Most of the others in the group had smarter jobs than me, more status, more money. There was only one other guy who was in an unskilled job like me. I thought they would all be smart Alecs but I realise now that I'm just as smart. We were working on some problem-solving activity Joseph had given us to do. The others seemed to be half-heartedly following a suggestion that one of them had made. But I had this idea to do it a different way, had made some notes and had almost blurted out that they were doing it wrong but something held me back. I didn't have the guts I think.

Joseph noticed my scribbles and asked me questions and got me talking about my idea. And hey presto, my idea was adopted! Everyone was enthusiastic about it and it worked out pretty well.

Stefania

I came to the UK from Romania only a few months ago, new country, new job and now, new study. Everything is new and I have to get used to it. You know, sometimes when people hear my accent and they ask me where I'm from, I think I feel a little worried to tell them. On the first day of my study Joseph asked us all to say something about ourselves and I was worried. I talked about my family and my home in Romania. But Joseph asked me many questions about myself, about my family and my life at home. This made me feel that my story was important; it made me feel welcome.

Hua

Joseph encouraged Tian and me to speak to each other in Mandarin when we were working as a pair. I was surprised but very pleased because it made me feel that my own language was accepted. For many Chinese people there is a feeling of inferiority connected to our history and China's relationship with Great Britain and a sense that our language is perhaps not valued as much as English.

Two issues are illustrated in these case studies. The first is to do with the potential barriers that group membership might pose for learners and the second is to do with the contribution that group membership might enable individual learners to make.

Critical thinking activity

» *What potential barriers to learning, specific to group membership, can you identify in the above comments? How have they been minimised?*

» *What contributions were the learners able to make because of their group membership? Can you think of any other examples?*

Some barriers are connected to age and status. Older learners such as Tony could feel anxious about appearing 'past it' in the eyes of the rest of the group and there is a very real fear among many older people that as they age, they are less able to learn. Some learners like Neil can feel threatened when it seems to them that the majority of their fellow learners are better than they are, for example they are better educated or in better jobs. They can lose confidence in their ability to participate.

Differences in culture and language can also create barriers. Learners such as Stefania and Hua could feel isolated and anxious because they are unfamiliar with British culture. Culturally specific language, for example when a politician is described as being on the 'left' or 'right' of a political party, can be particularly challenging for those not in the know. Technical words can also be a problem; it's unlikely, for example, you would know the meaning of the phrase 'functional skills' if you weren't in the teaching profession. The English language also contains a significant amount of idioms, useful in teaching because they can convey complex ideas quickly. But consider for example the complexity of meaning in the phrase 'throw the baby out with the bathwater'. Most people whose first language is English use idioms automatically and understand them implicitly. However, they are likely to be perplexing for those without the backdrop of British culture. The best option is to try to avoid using culturally specific language. This isn't all that easy to do but recognising its potential for creating barriers does at least give you the opportunity to explain meanings as situations arise.

Professional teachers who are curious about their learners are able to do more than anticipate and minimise barriers, important though this is; they are able to harness and celebrate what a learner can contribute simply because they are a member of a group. Joseph recognised that Tony and the two other older learners may well have had insights that would add to the discussions just because they *were* older. Learners often have much to teach both fellow learners and teachers, and it doesn't matter whether the group they belong to is based on culture, age, social/economic status or something else. Each of these can be celebrated in numerous ways, from simple shared histories and experiences to utilising skills and talents to solving problems and helping other learners.

Critical thinking activity: recognising diversity in practice

Consider the composition of a typical group of your learners.

» What potential barriers can you identify connected with their group membership?

» How might you celebrate the diversity within your group of learners?

A professional attitude

Teachers will need to be aware of how they are positioned and what their grounding/founding principles are in terms of the social, cultural, ethnic, religious and linguistic backgrounds of their students.

(Baker and Blair, 2008, p 34)

In the previous chapter you saw how personal values and emotions inform your professional relationships with learners and colleagues. The final section in this chapter on diversity is about your beliefs and assumptions about others. It provides an opportunity for you to look at your attitudes and your responses to different groups of learners and to decide if and how they inform your professional practice.

Imagine you have just picked up the class register for a new group of learners and as you read down the list, among the more typical first names, you see: Kyle, Cody, Vi, Jade, Cynthia. What might come into your mind? Perhaps you might see Vi as an older person or Cynthia as posh. Making these judgements is something that we all do. We pick up signs about others not only from their names but from what they are wearing, from their expression, posture, gestures, the sound of their voice and so on. We do it unconsciously and we use what we have learned to make judgements about them, to try and work out what sort of person they are.

Sometimes we interpret information about other people to form a general or stereotypical image of them based on our previous experience. It's a sort of shortcut to understanding others. For example, we might see a man with a vicious looking dog and think he is a thug because experience tells us that this is sometimes the case. We can use a variety of information to make these judgements, for example a person's interests ('trainspotters are boring'), their occupation ('traffic wardens are miserable'), or their ethnic group ('Afro-Caribbeans are good at dancing') and so on. In other words we make judgements about an individual based not on them as an individual but on the group they belong to. This means it is easy to make erroneous judgements; that a learner, for example, may/may not be able to easily manage a task because they are older/younger, vocal/quiet and so on.

Psychology suggests that these judgements we make are more intuitive than rational. According to the American psychologist Jonathan Haidt (2012), these judgements are not something we think about and weigh up consciously and rationally. On the contrary, they are more instinctive. In fact, Haidt suggests that we make these intuitive judgements instantly and reason afterwards, usually to search for evidence to justify them.

Why this should be the case is buried in our evolutionary past but we appear to be programmed to make assumptions about those who are different. Haidt describes it as

> *a kind of rapid automatic process more akin to the judgments animals make as they move through the world, feeling themselves drawn toward or away from various things.*
>
> (Haidt, 2012, p 61)

It also seems that we are naturally drawn to others who we see as similar to us. We find it more difficult to identify with people who we see as different or belonging to another group and much easier with people who are like us. Haidt calls this tendency 'groupishness'. This raises a potential problem. How easy is it to value and celebrate diversity if we have a natural sense of our own group? There's more; because our attitudes and judgements are based on instinct, they are, much like our values, difficult to detect. Doing so requires conscious effort. Yet this is exactly what you are required to do as a teacher. Teaching

> *is not only about the methods of teaching but also concerned with the being of teaching... The being of teaching... requires an examination of one's values in relation to a range of factors to do with one's world view... that teachers are no less affected by ist/phobic attitudes than other members of society is stating the obvious. In order to check such attitudes one has to acknowledge them.*
>
> (Baker and Blair, 2008, pp 26–27)

Teachers are expected not only to examine their attitudes but also to understand how they inform their practice. They are, for example, encouraged

> *to ask, to what extent is my action influenced by realistic knowledge of the individual... and not by prior knowledge of the ethnic group, special needs, gender or economic status/social class.*
>
> (Baker and Blair, 2008, p 27)

Finding the answer to this question that Baker and Blair have posed is clearly important for professional practice but how do you actually go about examining your attitudes? The language Baker and Blair use does offer some help here. In choosing to use words such as acknowledging, examining and checking, they are clearly thinking in terms of a process, something ongoing that takes a little thought and effort. Yet this shouldn't put you off. It is possible to see the process simply as two stages: identifying and modifying.

Think again about those intuitive responses that we all make. You will already have noted that we make these judgements instantly and use reason afterwards, usually to search for evidence to confirm our judgements. You may well see this process in action through your own responses to the following statements.

Critical thinking activity: part one – identifying attitudes

» *Read through the following statements. As you read each one, make a note of your initial response to it – one word or a short phrase is sufficient.*

a) *A 69 year-old lawyer plans to go to university to study medicine and become a general practitioner (GP).*

b) *Teenagers from poor backgrounds who wish to go to university are to be accepted with lower grades.*

c) *A number of schools in the UK offer a selection of GCSE subjects in the Polish language.*

» *Now, against each initial response, make any additional comments that come to mind about each of the statements.*

The chances are that your initial response would have been a gut reaction, feeling that each of these was in some way either a good or a bad idea. Your immediate response to the first statement, for example, may well have been 'good luck to him', an automatic, instinctive and intuitive judgement about a group of people – that it is right and acceptable that older people should have equal access to education. The thoughts that followed are likely to have been a rationalisation of your initial response, reasons to justify it. You may have added, for example, 'he should do well as he is already familiar with studying' or 'we need more doctors'. On the other hand, your initial response may have been something like 'He's too old' or 'Rather him than me!' If so, you might then have justified your response with 'He'll find it difficult to study effectively at this level' or 'He'll probably be dead before he does any work!'

The assumption in this critical thinking activity was that you justified your initial responses by searching for reasons to support them – what most of us tend to do most of the time. But this may not have been the case. You may instead have found that your initial response and your subsequent thoughts about one of more of the statements were, in fact, contradictory. Suppose for example that your initial response to the first statement was, 'He's too old' or 'Rather him than me!' But then, instead of looking for reasons to back this up, you began to question its validity. You may even have recognised that your immediate response was hasty and you then asked yourself, 'Why shouldn't an older person return to education and take up a new career later in life?' You may then have searched for evidence to support this alternative view, perhaps even engaging in a conversation with yourself putting forward a number of different viewpoints.

Sometimes, when turning things over in our minds we suddenly see things from a different perspective. It seems that even a couple of minutes of mulling something over can be enough to do the trick and give us a new perspective (Green and Paxton, cited in Haidt, 2012, p 69). This can be demonstrated by returning to those same statements and looking again at the processes you used to make your judgements.

Critical thinking activity: part two – modifying attitudes

» *Here are the statements again. Read through them and take a minute or two to reflect on each of them. Note if and how you have modified your view.*

a) *A 69 year-old lawyer plans to go to university to study medicine and become a GP.*

b) *Teenagers from poor backgrounds who wish to go to university are to be accepted with lower grades.*

c) *A number of schools in the UK offer a selection of GCSE subjects in the Polish language.*

This type of dispassionate logical analysis is not easy. If we are not challenged, we tend to hold on tenaciously to our beliefs. Yet if, in either part of this critical thinking activity, you did come to view one or more of those statements in a new light, you are doing exactly what is required of you, examining and modifying your attitudes. You are in fact demonstrating a number of the attributes that Jeanne Hitching (2008) suggests are necessary for what she calls a professional development mindset. These attributes include honest self-appraisal, reflective observation and professional curiosity. And this is perhaps one route to understanding our fundamental beliefs, to engage in honest reflective observation, to continually question those intuitive responses we all make and to search for alternative arguments and justifications.

Another well-tried and tested method of modifying attitudes is through honest, open debate, joining together with others and discussing issues around gender, race, age and so on. Friends and colleagues, for example, can challenge us and provide arguments that produce new ways for us to view old beliefs and assumptions.

Critical thinking activity: identifying and modifying attitudes in practice

» *Think about a number of your learners. Take each in turn and ask yourself the following questions.*

1. *Do I have any beliefs about this learner, or do I make any assumptions/ judgements based on their gender, age, faith, physical or mental characteristics, ethnicity, socio/economic status, disability, sexual orientation or something else?*

2. *Do my beliefs, assumptions or judgements inform my attitudes/responses to this learner and, if so, how?*

The contemporary British philosopher Colin McGinn (1991, p 104) calls the ability to arrive at informed and thoughtful moral judgements 'intelligence'. In his words, 'Oh how I wish I could put an end to stupidity! It and its fellow gang members: prejudice, narrow mindedness, ignorance, fear'. Yet McGinn isn't talking about something new and innovative. Far from it: from ancient times, from Confucius to Socrates to Kant, philosophy has recognised, understood and cherished this ability. But it wasn't known as intelligence; it was rightly acknowledged as wisdom.

Conclusion

As a professional teacher you are always learning, and your curiosity about your subject and about the learners you teach is a key feature of your professional practice. It enables you to support the needs of each learner and to celebrate the diversity of your teaching groups. Another key feature of your professionalism is your desire for self-knowledge, and the best tool to hand to achieve it is that of reflective self-analysis. As Baker and Blair (2008) point out, reflection has as much to do with 'being' as it has to do with methods. Central to *being* are the attitudes, beliefs and intuitive responses that inform your relationships with your learners.

Chapter reflections

» *Professional curiosity enables you to build relationships with learners that best support their individual needs.*

» *Professional curiosity helps you to value diversity and promote inclusion.*

» *Through honest debate and reflective observation you can identify and modify your assumptions and judgements.*

Taking it further

Appleyard, N and Appleyard, K (2009) *The Minimum Core for Language and Literacy*. Exeter: Learning Matters.
Although primarily concerned with issues of literacy, this book examines many of the background factors that affect adult learners, including influences and attitudes, participation, barriers and diversity.

Cole, M (2008) *Professional Attributes and Practice: Meeting the QTS Standards*. Abingdon: Routledge.
In the introductory chapter to this book Cole puts forward a five-step plan for examining what he calls phobias or isms, for example sexism or racism.

Hitching, J (2008) *Maintaining Your Licence to Practise*. Exeter: Learning Matters.
Jeanne Hitching, a member of the Institute for Learning Strategy Group, writes clearly and concisely on a number of different aspects of professionalism.

References

Ashmore, L, Dalton, J, Noel, P, Rennie, S, Salter, E, Swindells, D and Thomas, P (2010) Equality and Diversity, in Avis, J, Fisher, R and Thompson, R (eds) *Teaching in Lifelong Learning: A Guide to Theory and Practice*. Maidenhead: OU Press.

Baker, C and Blair, M (2008) High Expectations, Achieving Potential and Establishing Relationships, in Cole, M (eds) *Professional Attributes and Practice*. London: Routledge.

Haidt, J (2012) *The Righteous Mind*. London: Penguin.

Hitching, J (2008) *Maintaining Your Licence to Practise*. Exeter: Learning Matters.

LLUK (2007) *New Overarching Professional Standards for Teachers, Tutors and Trainers in the Lifelong Learning Sector*. London: LLUK.

McGinn, C (1992) *Moral Literacy*. London: Gerald Duckworth & Co. Ltd.

Rogers, J (2001) *Adults Learning*. Buckingham: OU Press.

Websites

www.bbc.co.uk/religion (last accessed 6 February 2014)

www.multifaithcentre.org (last accessed 6 February 2014)

5   The proof of the pudding is in the teaching

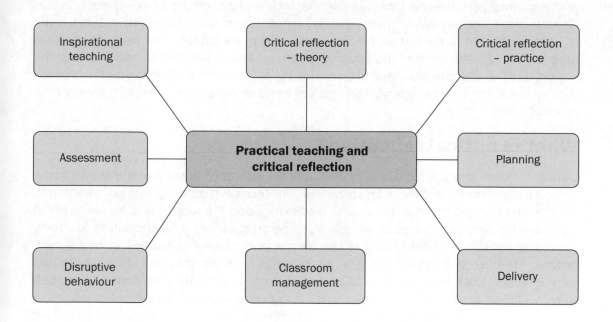

Chapter aims

This chapter will help you to:

- understand the concept of critical reflection;

- analyse how critical reflection can be applied to practical teaching;

- critically reflect on your own teaching;

- aspire to teaching excellence.

Introduction

This is where it all comes together. All the features of professionalism covered in the previous chapters – self-awareness, an understanding and interest in learners, curiosity and a love of the subject – come to fruition in teaching. This is the stage at which professionalism is demonstrated; in planning, classroom management, motivating learners, assessing learning and evaluating performance. However, this chapter – and indeed this book – is not primarily about how to teach effectively. There are many excellent books that cover this in detail, some of which are listed in the further reading at the end of the chapter. Rather the emphasis here is on how the features of professionalism are evident in practical teaching. One of the key skills of the effective professional teacher is the skill of critical reflection that permeates their whole approach to teaching. This chapter looks at professional teaching through the prism of critical reflection.

What is critical reflection?

During the latter years of his rule Marcus Aurelius, Emperor of Rome and the known world, wrote a series of notes and reminders to himself. The focus of his jottings was self-awareness. He examined his perceptions, his values, his feelings and the judgements he made about those around him. He reflected on his role as emperor, questioning his responses to others, reminding himself to speak simply to the Senate and cautioning himself to be tolerant, flexible, objective and open-minded in his dealings with his courtiers. Marcus' jottings were intended to be read only by himself, but against all odds, they survived and in 1559 were published under the title 'Meditations'. If you were to read Marcus' notes you would immediately recognise that he was a natural reflective practitioner and what you had in front of you was a very early reflective journal (Hays, 2003).

The concept of critical reflection

At first glance critical reflection appears to be a simple-enough concept. When you are having a welcome cup of coffee after a lesson you naturally think about how that lesson had gone. 'Should I have challenged Sophie when she came in late and didn't apologise? The Q/A session went quite well but I had to postpone the feedback until next week. Why did everyone get confused when I was explaining how the new software worked?' All these thoughts are reflective and at least imply self-criticism. But there is more to critical reflection than just having passing thoughts about a particular lesson, and the concept has been the subject of many studies of professionalism in recent years.

A good starting point is the work of David Kolb (1983) on experiential learning. His model describes a process in which a professional reflects on a specific incident, and then uses experience and understanding to decide how to act in future. Later, they put this plan into operation and evaluate the result. The cycle then starts again with the practitioner reflecting on how the new approach has worked and so the cycle repeats continuously in a progressive spiral. So if you were teaching the tardy Sophie mentioned above, you might try talking to her after the class the next time she is late and see if this improves her timekeeping and, if so, it might be a useful technique to use in similar situations.

Another influential writer on professional reflective practice is Donald Schön (1983) with his concepts of different types of theoretical knowledge and distinct modes of reflection. He distinguishes between two modes of reflection. Reflection *on* action is reflection that takes place when you are thinking back on how a lesson has gone – the coffee-break thoughts outlined above. But there is also reflection *in* action, the immediate, almost instinctive response to an unforeseen incident during a lesson. In this scenario professionals draw automatically upon their repertoire of skills, knowledge and experience to change their plan and respond to a new situation. Postponing feedback to a Q/A session because of lack of time is a straightforward example of reflection in action.

Schön sees a similar duality in his ideas about educational theory. He identifies two types of theory. Firstly, there are espoused theories – the established theories that form the basis of teacher training programmes. Then there are theories in use, your own ideas about teaching that you form with classroom experience. Schön's point was that both types of theory are important and valid for a professional, and that as your experience increases, so does the amount of theory in use that you draw upon.

Stephen Brookfield (1995) develops this strand of thought in his concept of critical lenses, by which he means those different points of view that professionals need to consider in their approach to teaching. In addition to established theory (espoused theory in Schön's terms) and your own view as a professional (theory in use) the views of your learners and your colleagues also need to be taken into account. The implication here is that there needs to be some way of finding out what these views are. Otherwise, you may well make assumptions about, for example, the best teaching methods to use with your learners without taking into account different learning styles. One of the strengths of this model is that it discourages an inward-looking absorption and encourages the professional to talk to colleagues, learners and others about professional issues.

A more recent model has been proposed by Gary Rolfe et al. (2001), who defines reflective practice in terms of a very simple cycle of three questions: 'What? So what? Now what?'

- The first question ('What?') requires an objective analysis and definition of the situation or event being considered. In the scenario at the start of this section you reflected over a cup of coffee on one of your lessons where your learners became confused when you were talking about new software.

- 'So what?' is a consideration of the consequences of an event for you as a teacher and for your learners. What does the event tell you about your actions? What was the effect on your learners? In the scenario the consequence could be that your learners weren't able to do the exercises and became fractious. Perhaps you tried to rush the topic or assumed they were more familiar with the programme than you had anticipated.

- 'Now what?' requires you to think about other approaches you could have used. What do you need to do to make things better and what are the likely consequences? In the scenario, the topic may need to be done again in simpler terms and with more time allowed the following week.

Critical thinking activity: the concept of critical reflection

» *Use the internet and library resources to research academic models of critical reflection. In addition to the authors mentioned above, you may find the work of Graham Gibbs (1988) and Chris Johns and Dawn Freshwater (2005) useful. Which of these models is helpful to your own reflective practice? Why is this so?*

Features of critical reflection

One of the noticeable features of these models of reflective practice is that, although there is significant difference of emphasis, there is a considerable amount of overlap and common ground. It seems that key features include the following.

- *A cyclical system.* Critical reflective practice is not something that starts one day and ends a few days later when a satisfactory outcome is achieved. Neither is it something that you do at the start of your professional career and stop doing when you gain a bit of experience. It is an ongoing process of action, reflection, revised action, more reflection and more revised action that becomes an almost instinctive tool to improve your professional practice throughout your career.

- *Learning from a wide variety of sources.* The truly professional practitioner doesn't depend on one source of learning. Theoretical knowledge and understanding can be important but are not exclusive sources. Drawing on your own practical experience is likely to become an increasingly important technique as your career progresses. Comment and advice from others – colleagues, mentors, line managers, your learners – will also be an important source of learning for your professional practice.

- *A logical and objective analysis.* Most of the models identify a systematic sequence of analysis with the following stages:

  - Choose and describe an event or dilemma. 'I couldn't get the class to work in groups. All they did was argue and chat about what they were going to do after the class.'

  - Identify possible explanations of why the problem arose – *reflection*. 'I didn't brief them properly. There wasn't enough time to get the project finished. They were fed up after a hard day.'

  - Identify what you could do to avoid the situation in future – *reflection and action*. 'Give a briefing handout so they are clear what they have to do. Tell them the ground rules for group work and have a discussion about these rules before getting involved in the project. Reschedule the project and do it earlier in the day.'

- – Put your ideas into practice – *action*. 'Design briefing sheet. List ground rules on whiteboard. Plan next project for 9am session.'
- – Analyse how the revisions went – *reflection*. 'Discussion on ground rules was very successful, and most of the group seemed to appreciate being able to negotiate. Briefing sheet missed out the hand-in date and had two spelling errors!'

And so the cycle continues, hopefully resulting in a continuing improvement in professional understanding and practice and in more effective teaching.

- • *The importance of recording your reflections.* It is very easy to have a blinding insight after you have finished a lesson and then forget about it. Most models stress the importance of capturing your reflections in a regular and systematic way, typically in the form of a reflective journal. This is more than a personal diary that just records what has happened and how you feel about it. The journal will also include your thoughts on how to solve the problems, why you think your revised strategy might work and what actually happened when you put your new plan into action. The format of your journal is not important. What matters is that it becomes a regular, almost instinctive activity, as much a part of your professional practice as planning your lessons.

To summarise, the reflective practitioner is a permanent learner, engaged in a continual process that illustrates a self-critical, collaborative and creative attitude.

Examples of critical reflection

The ability to reflect critically is a skill that gets better with practice. Here are two examples taken from the journals of teachers at the beginning of their careers, one reflecting on his presentation skills, the other reflecting on her lack of confidence.

CASE STUDY

Reflecting on presentation skills: Paul

Paul is studying for a Cert Ed and is employed by a private training agency. Here is an early extract from his reflective journal in which he concentrates on how he presented his material to his learners.

The things I concentrated on in this session were my presentation techniques. Right at the beginning I made sure I explained goals and targets, how the sessions would be organised and what I would like the learners to do. I also made sure I had their attention, was careful to think about speaking clearly, pausing and emphasising key words to reinforce important points and to signpost what was coming. I'm also remembering to explain the more technical bits and use the whiteboard to back them up. I find it takes all my concentration to think about varying the pace and tone of my voice to show my enthusiasm and to make it interesting, while moving my gaze around so that everyone feels included. And do it all at the same time as thinking about what I'm saying – it's a lot but I'm getting there.

This morning I was giving them a briefing on their project. It's pretty straightforward as it is the first one but I took it carefully and backed it up with a handout. I suggested they might want to have a go at their project plan, write the first part of the report and I would have a look at it and give them some feedback. Ellie asked if she could give her project any title she wanted and Clare wanted to know how much time they had to do it. I listened carefully to their questions, without interrupting and then repeated them to the whole class before answering so everyone knew what had been asked. At the end I checked that everyone understood by asking the class if they knew what they had to do and they all seemed to be fine. So, all in all I'm very pleased with how it went.

There is not much in this extract that is reflective, and nothing that can be described as critical. It is essentially a factual description of what Paul was concentrating on and how he tried to put his thoughts into action. He was therefore surprised and disappointed when he met the class next time, as seen by his next journal entry.

CASE STUDY

Reflecting on presentation skills: Paul (continued)

I thought they were all fine, that they'd understood the briefing but I was wrong. When I got their work back too many of them had not done what I'd asked them to. Some had completely misunderstood what I'd said and had not done the plan; others had done the whole thing instead of just the first part. Next time I need to make sure they really understand by asking more questions and getting them to explain how they are going to tackle it. And next time I definitely won't rely on them actually reading the handout – half of them had lost it anyway.

I'm beginning to understand that presentation skills are not just about talking. I need to spend a lot of time interacting with the learners, explaining, questioning, advising, listening and so on. I certainly realise that what you say to learners is not necessarily what they hear and understand. They will understand what I say in a way that makes sense to them, in other words, what they think I mean. I'm going to have to choose my words carefully and say the same thing in a different way, perhaps lots of different ways.

This extract is a lot more reflective. Paul has realised that teaching is about managing or facilitating as well as about performing ('I'm beginning to understand that presentation skills are not just about talking'). He has cottoned on to the need to get feedback to ensure everyone is on the same wavelength and to listen to what learners say, noting what he hears and sees as a valuable source of feedback ('I need to spend a lot of time interacting with the learners, explaining, questioning, advising, listening and so on'). He now has a better awareness of the effect his words and how he said them had on his learners and how easy or difficult he made it for his learners to understand what he wanted from them. Overall, his journal entry shows that he has reflected on what went wrong and identified what he needs to do to put it right in future.

CASE STUDY

Reflecting on confidence: Asa

Asa is a newly qualified teacher working in a large FE college. Here is an extract from her reflective journal in which she writes about her lack of confidence in dealing with a boisterous class.

I felt very anxious at first about this new class. I kept on thinking, "Will I forget what I'm supposed to be saying? Will they listen?" But I got a good tip from Jane, who is a really experienced teacher. She said that if you feel anxious one good way is to fake it; just pretend you're confident. So this morning I tried to imagine myself as a confident teacher; I imagined what I might look like and what I'd do – or not do. I saw myself:

- *making eye contact with everyone;*

- *smiling – showing that I wanted to be there;*

- *keeping my voice steady;*

- *standing up straight, but relaxed;*

- *not separating myself from the learners.*

So I tried it this morning and it seemed to work! It really is possible to pretend to be that confident person. Of course, it didn't work out quite as well in reality as it did in my imagination but I know it helped me to feel more confident. And even if I wasn't feeling quite as confident as I appeared to be, at least I looked the part. It seems that it isn't necessary to actually feel confident only to appear to be confident.

This is a reflection on the part of someone trying out something new and discovering it worked. The techniques Asa listed are specific and observable, and this clearly is something that will help her build on her new-found confidence. Her source was a colleague, but the conclusions are well established in theory, as Asa went on to discover, as seen from a subsequent entry in her journal.

CASE STUDY

Reflecting on confidence: Asa (continued)

I found it fascinating that visualising myself as a confident teacher can help to quell my nerves so I decided to find out more about it. I read about sportspeople visualising themselves running faster, jumping higher or hitting the ball accurately, a sort of dress rehearsal for the real thing. Apparently the brain finds it difficult to distinguish between visualising and memory. So, having set the mental scene a few times it becomes familiar and your brain recognises the experience, so when you do it for real you already know what's expected. There's a book on teaching by Jeanne Hitching that suggests you can take this idea further and copy the mannerisms of people you see who display a particular desired behaviour, for example, the way they speak, their gestures, their posture and so on.

This extract is a good example of how reflection is cyclical. Asa has reflected on her insight that appearing to be confident works for her. She has found out more about confidence-building techniques that she can try out and then reflect again on how effective they are. Also, she is using a variety of sources to confirm her initial impressions. Hints from an experienced colleague have now been supplemented by theory. Brookfield's critical lenses have been put to practice.

Critical thinking activity

» *To what extent do Paul's and Asa's journal extracts represent effective critical reflection of their professional practice?*

Reflecting on your teaching

As you have just seen, critical reflection is more than randomly thinking about what has happened during a lesson. There is a need for some sort of structure so that your analysis is objective, comprehensive and logical; in short it needs to be professional.

A good starting point is to look again at the key features of professionalism that have been identified in the previous chapters and that could be included in any list as relevant criteria for evaluating your teaching. You might feel that the following should be included:

- awareness of your own values, virtues, beliefs and emotions and how they influence your teaching;
- knowledge and understanding of your learners, both as individuals and members of the group;
- ability to establish an inclusive and professional relationship with your learners, and a learning environment characterised by trust and respect;
- subject expertise: knowledge, theoretical understanding and practical skill;
- teaching expertise: practice underpinned by theory shown in planning, delivery, classroom management, use of resources, assessment and evaluation;
- enthusiasm for your subject and for learning combined with a desire for your learners to share this enthusiasm.

Critical thinking activity

» *To what extent do these points represent a comprehensive list of criteria for critically evaluating your teaching? Add any further criteria that you feel are needed to give an accurate picture of your professional teaching situation.*

Professional teachers in action

This section contains extracts from the reflective journals of five different FE teachers. When reading them through, note the extent to which they meet the criteria you have devised for evaluating teaching professionalism.

CASE STUDIES

Teachers in action

1. Lesson planning

Sarah, Lecturer in History and Politics, FE college

GCSE History class

I think I'm going to have to change the way I plan my lessons with the GCSE History group as the last couple of lessons on the First World War have not been a roaring success. At present I'm using the college lesson plan proforma that has the standard headings: Time – Teacher activity – Learner activity – Resources – Assessment – Evaluation, and it's too restrictive.

The main problem is the diversity of the group. All 12 of them are really keen and interested, especially the boys when we talk about the fighting. But both Jade and Andrea are so slow that I think the others are giving up on them and don't like them in their small discussion groups. I've tried to vary the methods, but there's no getting away from the fact that the two girls seem to learn in a different way; they like finding things out for themselves and much prefer to work on their own and at their own pace. They're happy enough to catch up in their own time; it's just that they don't like the pressure of being chivvied along by the boys in the group.

So I need to differentiate, not by outcome (they all need to do the same project to be marked under the same criteria) but maybe by varying the learning activities to suit individuals. For instance, if I got the group to work in pairs I could pair Andrea and Jade together and let them do some research in the library rather than relying just on the stuff I give in handouts. At least it might ease the frustration I'm beginning to sense in the class.

I think it's worth a try, but I need to amend the plan to show that these two are doing the work in a different way. Perhaps a separate column heading to show this. If it works there may be mileage in doing this with some of my other classes.

2. Programme delivery

Khaled, Training Officer, Pharmaceutical company

Induction course for new employees

I know that induction courses aren't the most exciting of courses, but I think they're really important. If they work well the new employees begin to feel they belong to a supportive community and it makes a big difference to how they see the organisation. So for me it's important to make the day interesting and have a happy bunch of people at the end.

I'm really pleased with the way the course went today. The best bit was the first session. Instead of the usual 'Go around the room and say something about yourself' routine, I divided them into pairs and asked them to interview each other for five minutes and then tell the whole group what they had found out. They really enjoyed it, everyone found a new friend and it set a relaxed and chatty tone for the rest of the day. It took longer than I estimated but was well worth it for setting the right tone.

Another good thing was to use the conference room for the first time instead of the old training room. It helped me because I was able to use the new interactive whiteboard and being in posh surroundings helped to make the new people feel valued. I also stayed with them in the coffee breaks, and was surprised how many minor bits of confusion I was able to clear up, so I'll do that again.

Not everything is right yet though. There's still too much input and not enough time for discussion. Too much time going through the staff handbook; next time I'll send it out with the joining instructions and get them to read it in advance, then we can discuss important bits on the course rather than tediously going through page by page.

And I've got to do something about Walter, the Safety Officer, who just reads his notes and is so monotonous that he sends them all to sleep. Maybe persuade him to show that video he's made and just have a bit of a Q and A session afterwards.

Everyone filled in their happiness sheets at the end, and they seem OK, so I won't get the sack just yet!

3. Classroom management

Francesca, Lecturer in Business Management, large FE college

HNC Management course (Marketing module)

I'm having problems with this group. Today was my second session and I'm beginning to sense that Tony, Graham and Ahmed think they know more about marketing than I do. They all work in Sales and seem to think I'm just an academic in an ivory tower who knows the theory but has never done the hard graft. It also doesn't help because I think Graham resents being taught by a woman, and seems really reluctant to engage in any sort of meaningful discussion with me. It all comes out in fairly aggressive responses when I ask him questions and I overheard some fairly misogynist coffee-break comments when he didn't realise I was in earshot. It made me angry and I had to bite my tongue and not provoke a confrontation. In itself this isn't too serious, but I'm worried that it could affect the rest of the group, particularly Jane who is the only other woman in the class and is a bit reluctant to contribute.

So what to do about it? Some options:

- *Take Tony, Graham and Ahmed aside, explain that marketing is a lot more than sales and that experience without an understanding of theory will always limit them. Otherwise, why bother coming on the course?*

- *Ignore their behaviour, but ensure they are split up when allocated to syndicate work?*

- *Talk to Graham and say that sexist comments are unacceptable?*

- *Talk to the whole group and make clear what I think is unacceptable behaviour?*
- *Talk more about my own marketing experience in Spain?*

4. Dealing with disruptive behaviour

Wesley, Lecturer in Functional Skills, College of Agriculture

Diploma in Land-Based Studies (Effective Communication module)

Well, this morning was a baptism of fire! Taught my first session on Communication Studies with the level 2 diploma group in place of Gina who's just gone on maternity leave. Arrived ten minutes early for the 9am session and nobody else arrived until 9.10, when Charley and Pauline wandered in. Apparently the whole group had had a heavy night at someone's birthday party and by 9.20 I'd still only got 12 out of 15. What was worrying was that nobody apologised – sloppy timekeeping seems par for the course with this lot.

When we eventually got started, Hailey's mobile phone rang and she was really sullen when I told her to turn it off. This led to a rancorous discussion with some of the class who said Gina let them keep phones on in case of emergencies. While this was going on, Jody got out his copy of The Sun and started reading it and had the nerve to say, 'Well, it's communication, innit!' when I told him to put it away. By this time I was very irritated. I'd had enough and told them to go away for a ten-minute break, but when they came back I'd need to talk to them about what was acceptable and what was not in my classes.

They came back more or less on time, but all a bit sullen. When I said I wanted to make a sort of contract with them about what they expected from me and what I should expect from them at least they listened and we had a reasonable discussion. What became very clear was that they really wanted to learn about farming and do the practical stuff like driving tractors, and saw communication as a distraction from what really interested them; just a mixture of grammar and boring report writing according to Charley. They clearly didn't see Gina's classes as a bundle of fun!

In the end I said that I'd bring some suggestions about what we should do next time, but that we could negotiate. But they had to come on time and turn their phones off! So I've got some work to do to link my input to their other classes. I'll need to talk to the other tutors as well.

5. Assessment

David, Lecturer in Travel and Tourism, FE college

BTEC Travel and Tourism course

I've got a problem with Syed because he's just complained about the C+ grading I've given him for his second project (report on identifying a new Mediterranean resort for an upmarket travel company). He reckons I've marked him too severely because I've penalised his English and not given enough credit for his research. The thing is that he has seen Samantha's assignment which has a B grade and I've commented on her script that she has missed out the section on transport links that Syed has done very well. His point is that this is not an English test and that he has covered all the issues asked for in the brief and therefore deserves at least as good a grade as Samantha. And it matters to him because although this is a formative assessment he feels it might be taken into account in his end-of-course grading.

I've looked at both scripts again and think he may actually have a point. His sentence structure and punctuation are really poor but he has covered all the points. The problem is that although the marking guide has criteria requiring good presentation, layout, grammar and punctuation it does not give a weighting to this. I emphasised at the start that they should imagine their report would be considered by senior management and Samantha's presentation was really excellent. And should I have taken into account that English is not Syed's first language? I wonder if my judgement has also been influenced by the fact that Samantha's first assignment was outstanding and I expected her to get another A grade this time, whereas I didn't have the same expectations of Syed? And also if I upgrade Syed, I might be opening the door for others in the class to complain.

I think I'll tell Syed that I'll ask Pauline, the Travel Geography lecturer, to second mark his script, so that we can get a neutral view of his work. For the longer term, at the next team meeting I'll raise the issue of giving specific weightings for each element of the marking schedules for this course. At least it should ensure better reliability. But also I think we should have a discussion about validity – in this case how valid is it to give a grade for report writing for a project which essentially assesses research skills and knowledge of a particular travel destination?

Critical thinking activity

» *What features of professionalism (or lack of it) can you identify from each of these reflective journal extracts? To what extent do these teachers meet your criteria for professional practice?*

To a greater or lesser extent, all these journal entries reflect some critical analysis of professional practice. They all, for example, describe a problem and suggest ways that the situation might be improved in future. Examples of this are Sarah's idea to pair off Andrea and Jade so that they can focus on the task and David's plan to have Syed's work reviewed by Pauline.

In terms of self-awareness, there are several examples of the teachers questioning their own attitudes and emotions and the effect the expression of these feelings is having on their learners. Francesca became angry and had to bite her tongue when she overheard sexist comments. David wondered if he had been influenced by Samantha's and Syed's previous work. The tone of both these comments is thoughtful, with the writers considering the effect of their feelings on their learners. By contrast, Wesley's comment that he became very irritated by his learners' behaviour and told them to go away seems far more self-centred and uncritical, with little indication that he appreciates the effect of his anger on his learners.

There are also several instances in these extracts to show that the writers understand their learners, both as individuals and members of a group. Sarah worries about the diversity of her group, how to meet the learning needs of Jade and Andrea without affecting group cohesion. Francesca has a pretty good understanding of what lies behind the aggressive behaviour of the three recalcitrant learners in her Marketing class; they feel that they know more about the subject than she does and Graham resents being taught by a woman. Khaled's comments show that he well understands the anxieties of a group of new learners coming together for the first time.

This appreciation of the learners' individual and group needs leads on to evidence of an inclusive and professional relationship with them. Khaled's enthusiasm for his ice breaker that ensured everyone found someone to talk to is an example of this, as is his use of a management suite so that his learners would feel valued. Sarah is concerned that she must differentiate so that all the learners in her diverse group are catered for while David is anxious that his learners should feel that they are being fairly assessed.

All the teachers in these scenarios are clearly experienced, with an understanding of the theory and practice of teaching. They all plan their lessons, use a wide range of resources, manage their classes, deal with disruptive behaviour with varying degrees of competence, assess learning and evaluate their performance in a self-critical way. They all possess a considerable level of subject expertise, and it is interesting that Francesca worries about her credibility with her learners now that she no longer is actively engaged in a marketing role.

Enthusiasm for their subject and for learning is at least implicit in all these scenarios. Sarah worries that the First World War does not interest at least a couple of her learners; it is important to Khaled that his induction course is successful and enjoyable; Francesca and Wesley worry that disruptive behaviour will hinder learning; and David is keen to ensure that assessment problems are solved so that his learners can concentrate on the next stage of their course. However, it is difficult to analyse enthusiasm in the same way that you can analyse a lesson plan or an assessment schedule. Indeed, enthusiasm is a key feature of professional teaching performance that deserves further consideration.

Professionalism and inspiration

Most judgements of teaching performance are based on completion of some form of checklist. In this way lesson observers (maybe including your learners!) are given a structure that ensures all the criteria for a good professional teaching performance are covered. You can use such a checklist to evaluate your own teaching performance; just complete it at the end of a lesson to identify the things that were successful and the problems you encountered, as a prelude to identifying how you would change things next time. It should not be too difficult to design your own checklist to cover the criteria you have established. In any event, many organisations have designed observation checklists as part of their quality assurance system, and many books on teaching in FE include such lists, such as Avis et al. (2010) and Hitching (2008).

The premise upon which such lists are based is that teaching is a skill that can be analysed and broken down into segments that can then be observed and evaluated. If all the boxes are ticked then you have an effective teaching performance. This is certainly a convincing argument concerning teaching competence. It is a bit like the driving test; if you can accomplish a safe emergency stop, execute a good three-point turn and demonstrate an ability to perform all the other components of the test to the required standard then you are competent enough to be given a licence to drive. Yet professionalism is more than meeting a minimum standard of competence; it is about excellence, high-quality and continuous development, and sometimes this is more difficult to analyse. This point can be illustrated by the story of Megan, a senior teacher in Catering at a large FE college.

CASE STUDY

Megan's teaching observations

Megan has recently been appointed as curriculum leader for the professional cookery courses at her multi-site college. One of her responsibilities is to observe and grade the teaching of all the full-time staff in her section for at least one lesson per semester as part of the college's quality assurance scheme. After observing two of her teachers she made the following comments in her journal, so that she could discuss the issue with her tutor on her masters degree.

I've just observed Gemma teaching the C & G Professional Cookery Diploma group over at the Newbridge site and it's been a really interesting experience, mainly because of the contrast between her teaching and Declan's class that I saw last week – he teaches a similar class but here on the main site. By coincidence, they were both covering costing and menu planning, so it's easy to compare.

I gave Declan a Grade 1 (outstanding) because quite frankly I couldn't fault him. His planning was excellent – clear and achievable outcomes, lots of variety for learner activity, clear progression and checking of progress, a wide range of resources and he gave concise pen-pictures of each learner that showed he knew them and understood their individual needs. As for the session itself, it was really well managed. Declan has a relaxed style, clearly knows his stuff and the learners were keen to work and enjoyed the tasks he set them. He was very good at using Q/A to regain someone's attention and to check their understanding, particularly the more complicated bits about costing. He managed group work very effectively, only intervening when he saw someone's attention wandering but letting the learners get on with solving the problems while their mind was on the task. All his resources – handouts, a short PowerPoint presentation, briefing sheets, etc. – were clear and well prepared. He was sensitive enough to depart from his plan when he realised that the menu-planning session needed extra time, and his own feedback to the learners' previous homework was detailed and supportive. In summary, he ticked all the boxes; I saw a highly professional teaching performance that the learners enjoyed and in which the learning outcomes were clearly achieved.

I also gave Gemma a Grade 1, but for a different reason. For a start, her lesson wasn't faultless. There were a couple of spelling mistakes on one of her handouts, and her lesson plan was a bit scruffy. But the striking thing about this lesson was there was a sense of excitement about it – difficult to generate when you're dealing with costing meals! Gemma's lessons were clearly the high point of this group's week; they loved being there and were so keen to learn that it seemed as if they felt they would be letting Gemma down if they didn't succeed. I spoke to Harry, one of the group, who told me that Gemma's classes had changed his life, and instead of just passing time at college to avoid being on the dole he was now determined to become a famous chef. What I'm trying to get my head around is to identify what it is about Gemma and her teaching that can create this buzz in her lessons and inspire an ordinary group of learners in such a way.

On reflection, I think there are a couple of things to note. Firstly, there was the relationship Gemma had with each learner and with the group as a whole. She has the rare gift of not only caring for her learners, but showing she cares throughout the lesson. You gained the impression that each learner felt that, when Gemma spoke to them, they were the most important person in the world at that moment, and that she was so concerned about their problem that she would do anything to help. At the same time she clearly had high expectations of all her learners, as was seen by the standard of work I saw. They clearly took pride in their assignments and a couple I spoke to seemed almost surprised about what they had managed to achieve since they started in Gemma's cookery class.

The second thing was Gemma's enthusiasm for professional cooking. Her excitement, even for her learners designing menus that she must have seen hundreds of times before was obvious and infectious. It's clearly founded on a wealth of experience as a chef, but somehow her demeanour in the classroom transmits an enthusiasm for her profession that is difficult to resist. She is passionate about her subject and delights in passing this on to others. All in all, I wish I had the personality and skills to create the learning atmosphere I witnessed in this session.

My problem is that this is difficult to convey by filling in our lesson observation forms, which are based on the premise that teaching can be broken down into a number of subsidiary skills and if each one gets a tick, hey presto you have an excellent teacher. I think that this approach gives you a record of a good, even excellent, professional performance but somehow you don't capture the synergy generated by an inspirational teacher.

Critical thinking activity

» *To what extent does an analytical evaluation of teaching give an accurate picture of professional practice?*

» *Is inspirational teaching a goal to which professionalism should aspire? Give reasons for your view.*

In the case study both Gemma and Declan showed enthusiasm for learning and for their subject and they both clearly cared about their learners, wanting them to share this enthusiasm. The difference seems to be that Gemma demonstrated these characteristics of professionalism to an extraordinary degree. Herein may lie the clue as to what defines an inspirational teacher. Bruce Marlowe (2006) cites the work of Richard Traina who analysed the biographies and autobiographies of prominent Americans to identify what these people saw as the traits of their best teachers.

There were three characteristics that were described time and again – to an astonishing degree: competence in the subject matter, caring deeply about students and their success, and character, distinctive character. These attributes were evident regardless of the level of education or the subject matter being taught.

1. *A command of subject matter, such that students picked up on the teacher's excitement about it, was fundamental. Where there was ease on the part of the teacher 'moving around the subject', a dexterity of explanation and explication, students could feel the teacher's command of the material. That confidence was a root cause of a student's respect for the teacher, opening the student up for learning – making the student more engaged. Autobiographers frequently cited teachers whose keen understanding of the subject matter caused students to see the world differently.*

2. *The second characteristic seemed equally important: caring deeply about each student and about that student's accomplishment and growth. In this instance, it began with the teacher recognising the student as an individual who brings particular experiences, interests, enthusiasms, and fears to the classroom. It was the teacher taking time to acknowledge a student's life outside the classroom... (and) it moved to an insistence that the student take pride in his or her work – stretching each person to a level of performance that surprised and delighted the student.*

3. *The third attribute, distinctive character, is the most elusive one, and it gives flavor or texture to the other two... It could be an unaffected eccentricity, a handicap or tragedy overcome, an unabashed passion for the subject, or a way of demonstrating concern for the student... In any event, there was a palpable energy that suffused the competent and caring teacher, some mark-making quality.*

I cannot emphasise enough how powerful this combination of attributes was... (Students) believed that their lives were changed by such teachers and professors.

(Marlowe, 2006, p 37)

Critical thinking activity: inspirational teaching

» *Do you agree with Traina's analysis of the characteristics of inspirational teachers?*

» *To what extent can a professional approach to teaching facilitate these characteristics?*

You may consider that it is all very well for outstanding individuals to become inspirational teachers, but it is a pretty tall order for normal people, however strongly motivated they may be. What this does provide, however, is a template, something that a professional can aim for throughout their career. It is a statement of the obvious that professional teachers aspire to excellence and that all would probably like to be recognised as an inspirational teacher as described by Richard Traina. One of the great things about a lifelong career as a teacher is that this quest never ends, and when things go well it is enormously rewarding. When you are elated rather than exhausted at the end of a lesson, when your learners have been excited and told you that they never really knew that your topic could be so interesting then maybe your professionalism is reaping its reward. The important thing is to try and capture what you did to generate such a rewarding feeling so that you can hopefully repeat it and embed it into your skill set. We are back to critical reflection again.

Conclusion

The main theme of this chapter is that critical reflection is the key to evaluating your teaching. To be effective, this reflective technique needs to be a continuous process undertaken throughout your professional career. It needs to be an objective analysis that encompasses the criteria for teaching excellence that are most appropriate for your particular job and career situation. It is concerned not only with identifying and seeking solutions to problems but also with identifying key reasons for success and embedding this into your teaching.

Chapter reflections

» *All the features of professionalism – self-awareness, an understanding and interest in learners, enthusiasm and a love of the subject – are demonstrated in your teaching.*

» *Critical reflection is a key element of your teaching, and can be used to evaluate how effectively the features of professionalism are developed in your professional practice.*

» *As a professional teacher you are a lifelong learner. The aim is to provide a standard of excellence in your teaching that you recognise from inspirational teachers.*

Taking it further

Hillier, Y (2002) *Reflective Teaching in Further and Adult Education*. London: Continuum.
This is an authoritative introduction to improving teaching skills through critical reflection.

Wallace, S (ed.) (2010) *The Lifelong Learning Sector Reflective Reader*. Exeter: Learning Matters.
This contains a comprehensive and detailed section (Chapter 7) on professionalism and reflective practice.

The following books are a sample of the wide range of publications that cover practical teaching skills in the FE sector.

Curzon, L (2002) *Teaching in Further Education*. London: Continuum.
Race, P and Pickford, R (2007) *Making Teaching Work*. London: Sage Publications.
Reece, I and Walker, S (2007) *Teacher Training and Learning*. Durham: Business Education Publishers.
Wallace, S (2007) *Teaching, Tutoring and Training in the Lifelong Learning Sector (4th edition)*. Exeter: Learning Matters.

References

Avis, J, Fisher, R and Thompson, P (2010) *Teaching in Lifelong Learning: A Guide to Theory and Practice*. Maidenhead: McGraw Hill Education.

Brookfield, S (1995) *Becoming Critically Reflective Teachers*. San Francisco: Jossey-Bass.

Gibbs, G (1988) *Learning by Doing: A Guide to Teaching and Learning Methods*. London: Further Education Unit.

Hays, G (2003) *Marcus Aurelius: Meditations*. London: Weidenfeld & Nicholson.

Hitching, J (2008) *Maintaining Your Licence to Practise*. Exeter: Learning Matters.

Johns, C and Freshwater, D [eds] (2005) *Transforming Nursing through Reflective Practice*. Oxford: Blackwell Science.

Kolb, D (1983) *Experiential Learning*. Englewood Cliffs, NJ: Prentice-Hall.

Marlowe, B (2006) *Educational Psychology in Context: Readings for Future Teachers*. London: Sage Publications.

Rolfe, G, Freshwater, D and Jasper, M (2001) *Critical Reflection for Nursing and the Helping Professions*. Basingstoke: Palgrave Macmillan.

Schön, D (1983) *The Reflective Practitioner: How Professionals Think in Action*. Aldershot: Ashgate.

6 The professional marketing specialist: branding the learning product

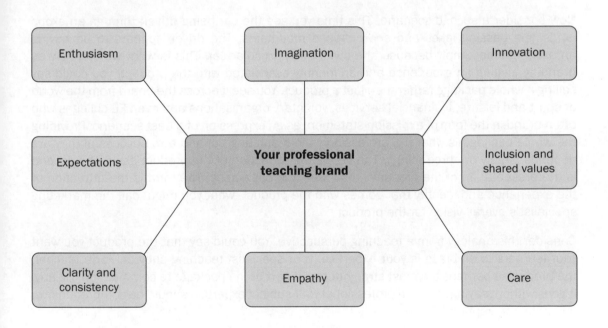

Chapter aims

This chapter will help you to:

- understand the concept of a teaching brand;
- review the range and characteristics of an effective teaching brand;
- identify and develop your personal teaching brand;
- identify the features of a best experience for learners.

Introduction

Imagine this scenario. You are thinking of purchasing a new car and are watching an advert on TV that shows a rather smart looking car; a voiceover describes the car's features: power, fuel economy, cup holders or whatever. The advert is comprehensive and informative; you learn a lot about the car.

Now consider a second scenario. This time you see the car being driven through an exotic landscape passing lakes and snow-capped mountains. The driver appears to be having an exciting time simply because she owns this particular car. This is what we all know as branding, selling an experience and an identity associated with the product; you could say selling a whole package rather than just a product. You see it across the board from the world of sport and leisure, to financial services, voluntary organisations and even FE colleges who often brand in the form of a mission statement as an expression of a best scenario. Providing the whole package is what the professionals in marketing do, and how successful they are depends largely on three things. The first is the attraction of the product itself. The second is the presentation of the product – how well it is put across. The third is the attraction of the experience and identity that comes with the product, what you might call the marketing specialist's overall vision for the product.

Consider this analogy from a teaching perspective. You could say that the product you want your learners to embrace is your expertise, your specialist teaching subject. For a teacher, the product is perhaps the most straightforward part of the package to comment on. Clearly, it goes without saying that as a professional your subject expertise should be comprehensive, accurate and kept up to date.

The second part of the package, presentation, is how well you get your subject across, your knowledge, skills and experience as a teacher. Your skills as a teacher in enabling your learners to learn will hopefully be along the lines of the examples of professional teaching in the previous chapter.

This leaves the final element in this package, the experience your learners have as part of their learning; you might call this your brand or your vision for learning. It is this element in the package that will be explored in this chapter, your own professional brand of teaching, as experienced by your learners.

Your brand: the learning experience you offer your learners

It might be said that a professional product and a professional performance would be more than enough to do a professional job. What more can anyone expect, over and above in-depth and current knowledge of your subject delivered with expertise? Yet consider again the marketing specialists. They are likely to know their product inside out and will also have well-honed delivery techniques. But these professionals know that these vital elements of the package won't in themselves be sufficient to do a professional job. They will, in addition, offer the potential customer the sort of experience that complements and enhances the product they are offering.

As a professional you will want to consider the brand you offer your learners, the experience that will complement and enhance your teaching product, the vision you have for your learners and for yourself. After all, you share your time and your classrooms/workrooms with learners. And once you have a vision clear in your mind, you will want to think about how you might pursue it.

There is no one right brand or learning experience any more than there is any right product brand.

> *Individual teaching styles reflect diverse elements driven by the psychological make-up of teachers, their formative experiences both as vocational and/or academic practitioners and often importantly, their attitude to their learners.*
>
> (Stott, 2010, p 3)

In essence, the experience that your learners have is largely one that stems from you as a professional teacher and as an individual with your personal values, virtues and beliefs. For this reason the vision you have for your learners will be unique. Make no mistake, it can take courage and commitment to pursue any vision, and teaching is certainly no exception – too often there is too much to do, and too little time to do it. Bureaucracy, paperwork and time pressures aside you are bound by other constraints, well summed up by the contemporary philosopher Julian Baggini.

> *On all fronts what teachers do is being judged against fixed, external measures. This means it is easy to believe that the teacher's professionalism is seen more in terms of how well they conform to these constraints, than in how well they display their own unique abilities or take decisions for themselves. For better or worse, a professional teacher must be able to work within these prescriptive limits and deliver results. This is perhaps the most demanding feature of professionalism in general.*
>
> (Baggini, 2005, p 10)

Against this backdrop you have to plan your way forward, to make your own judgements and create your own professional brand. Some parts of the learning package will be beyond your control. You are unlikely, for example, to be able to change the physical environment, or the degree of physical comfort of your learners. In addition, you have to work within the limitations of the communication systems and support services of your organisation. It would be great to have the luxury of operating without time constraints and to offer Costa-styled coffee breaks but you know how unlikely this is. However, physical and organisational constraints aside, the rest is yours. So how might you think about the nature of the experience you want for your learners and for yourself?

As a baseline from which you can develop your personal brand, one good place to start is the professional values set out in the LLUK Standards because here the learner is central to the values underpinning professional practice. Equally valuable to you as a guide are your own personal values and beliefs. It is a good idea here to review the section on values and virtues in Chapter 3 and you may even wish to reassess your responses to the critical learning activity, 'Identifying virtues in practice'.

Developing a professional teaching brand

In the previous chapter you looked at a case study that illustrated inspirational teaching as observed by a curriculum leader. That theme continues here with examples of how you might create and sustain a best learning experience for your learners. The following case studies illustrate different elements of a professional teaching brand but this time from the perspective of learners themselves. In each case study the teacher is passionate about teaching, about learning and learners, and each is narrated by a learner describing their own very individual experiences of learning, the environment in which their learning takes place and the relationships that develop with their teachers and/or their fellow learners.

Experiencing high expectations

CASE STUDY

Rachel

I'm at college in the second year of the C & G Diploma in Hairdressing. When I started my course I had no intention of staying longer than a few weeks just to show that I'd given it a good try and to keep my mum off my back – she didn't want me sitting around at home all day watching Jeremy Kyle. She said I had to find a job, do voluntary work or go to college. No chance of a job round here, and the charity shop idea stank. I didn't fancy college either as I found school was a real drag – I hadn't worked – none of us in my set of friends had and the teachers just got fed up with us always mucking around. Funny, one option I was seriously thinking about was getting pregnant, getting a flat of my own and living off benefits – it seemed to be about the one thing I could do and I'd have a baby of my own. A couple of my mates had done it and they seemed fine and their babies were really cute.

But I had to give college a go just to keep out of the way of my mum's nagging and here I am a year later, not only still here but really enjoying it. I've made some good friends on this course but it's mainly because of Anwar our teacher. I made it pretty obvious that first week that I wasn't really interested. I turned up late for class, made little effort and didn't bother to hand in any work. I expected Anwar to moan at me like they did at school but he didn't. Instead he'd keep asking me what I thought about this or that and when I bothered to think of an answer he said I had some interesting ideas and he was looking forward to reading the case studies I would be doing on my service users. I told him I couldn't think why and he said he thought I had some important stuff in my head just waiting to be written down. No one had said that before and it got me thinking, did I have good stuff in my head? Well it was a bit of a challenge I suppose and I actually put a bit of effort into the first case study and handed it in. When Anwar gave it back to me he didn't mess me around. He said there was a lot of room for improvement but it was great when he said he liked some of my ideas. It made me feel really pleased with myself. Anwar said I would get better if I wanted to – I did want to and I have. I can't wait to start work now – there's a new salon just opened that I would love to work in.

Critical thinking activity

» *Rachel was motivated to engage with her course because Anwar convinced her that he valued her opinions and he had high expectations of her. How else might you motivate a learner like Rachel?*

» *Think about a group of your learners. Can you identify which of them are motivated by intrinsic/extrinsic factors? Do you see any difference in their approach to their learning?*

» *Following her negative experience of school Rachel's success at her studies helped to increase her self-esteem and self-confidence. Can you identify any of your learners who have experienced failure at school? How might you increase their confidence, self-esteem and motivation?*

As you saw in Chapter 4 the majority of learners in FE want to be there and to do well. For some the motivation is *intrinsic*, they are curious, interested in the subject for its own sake; for others the rewards are *extrinsic*, the chance of a job or more money. A small minority may have little motivation to succeed, some having memories of school years involving constant failure. This unhappy experience limits the expectations they have of themselves to achieve; if they have failed in the past their expectation is that they will continue to fail. These learners can find it almost impossible to visualise their future, let alone plan for it; what they do see is a horizon bereft of options, and they need help to revise their expectations of themselves, to be convinced that there are possibilities and that they can succeed. The psychologist Denis Lawrence suggests that teachers' expectations of their learners affect how well they do.

> *In essence tutors who expect their students to make progress are likely to find this expectation self-fulfilling. Perhaps just as importantly, where tutors are doubtful about their students' potential this will be communicated and be self-fulfilling.*
> (Lawrence, 2000, p 63)

Of course, what Lawrence suggests doesn't apply only to learners with low motivation; it is just as important that all learners, even those who are highly motivated, are stretched and challenged and their opinions valued in order for them to sustain their motivation.

Sadly, there are learners who, no matter what you do or how hard you try, will remain uninterested, resentful, apathetic and unmotivated. The important thing to remember here

Toby's no pushover though. When I started this course I know I was a bit of a nuisance with my phone. Toby had told us that when we were doing theory stuff in class he expected us not to make calls and to go straight outside if we had to take one. At first I was pretty good but I started to get lazy and take advantage by answering as I got up. But Toby soon collared me. He said it interrupted the rest of the class so what he'd like me to do was turn my phone to silent mode and not to answer the call until after I'd left the room. I remember I got a bit huffy then – if I didn't answer my phone there and then they'd ring off, I'd miss the call and it might be important. Toby didn't get irritated back though, he just said he could see the phone was important to me so he wasn't going to ask me to turn it off. Then he repeated what he wanted me to do quietly and friendly like.

Critical thinking activity

» *What do you see are the personal qualities that support and enhance Toby's professional practice?*

» *Why do you think Toby didn't ask Tom to turn the phone off? Would you have acted differently? If so, why?*

Passion isn't necessarily the all-dancing, all-singing variety that you saw in the previous case study. Just as valid is its expression in quiet ways such as in clarity, consistency and reliability, in being available and approachable. Increasingly teachers are being required to take on the pastoral care of their learners, and a professional approach to offering advice and support can be summed up as one that is friendly, encouraging, supportive of learners' anxieties, but is clear and recognises limits and boundaries. In this case study Toby used this approach to manage the problem with Tom and his phone. He understood Tom's standpoint, and accepted his attachment to his phone, but he was clear about the expected outcome. He knew that his message to Tom was likely to be met with disapproval but was confident to pass it anyway.

Lawrence (2000) suggests that it is important to be your genuine self, to stay with what you believe in, with what is important to you even when, as sometimes happens, a learner may see things very differently. It is about recognising, acknowledging and accepting a learner's point of view without compromising your own and in having the confidence to respond appropriately.

Experiencing empathy, support and confidentiality

CASE STUDY

Nosheen

I'm doing a CIPD course in Human Resource Practice. I'm normally a very confident and outgoing person. I hold down a good job – I'm an IT consultant. I get on with other people and I have a good social life. But when it comes to writing, I have a mental block with punctuation and spelling. It makes studying quite difficult for me but I'm pretty skilled at camouflaging my shortcomings because I'd be embarrassed if others in the class knew. This is the first time I think I've really enjoyed studying and it is all because of Lola, the tutor. I began the course in my usual panic state, never volunteered to write anything down or on the board. What I was most concerned about though was handing in work for marking. I knew mine wouldn't be great – I could sort out some of the spelling with spellcheck but it's not as easy to do that with grammar and punctuation and I can't cope with asking anyone to check my work before I hand it in – it would be excruciating.

But what happened when Lola gave us the briefing for the first piece of work was a real surprise. She made a point of saying that she wanted to give us as much help as we needed with the writing side as well as the content, and then she said something really weird – she said most people have one problem or another with writing, hers was spelling. I couldn't believe it – a teacher who's poor at spelling – and admits it! She made it seem so normal and run of the mill instead of this huge ogre. This was almost enough to convince me that I'd be OK handing in my work – but not quite! When the work was due in the following week I panicked, of course, and made a feeble excuse – I think I said I'd left it at home. Rationally I knew it didn't make sense – I knew it was only going to delay the inevitable. But I wasn't thinking straight because I was in panic mode and just wanted to avoid the exposure and humiliation.

The delay was short-lived though, about ten minutes in fact, because at the end of the session Lola asked me if we could have a quick chat. She waited until everyone else was out of earshot and then said that I'd been looking a bit worried all afternoon and could she help. I reckoned she might have guessed what the problem was so I told her and it was OK. She looked at what I'd written and said lots of good things about it. Lola told me that there were things that needed to be worked on but there was time and she knew I would be able to manage it. She said she would sort out some help straight away to get me started. Then she made me laugh by telling me about a time she'd messed up a very important presentation because she'd made a couple of stupid spelling errors and hadn't checked beforehand – someone in the audience pointed them out and she wanted the floor to open up and swallow her whole. It was then that I knew there was no way anyone else in the class would get to know about my problem with spelling and punctuation – she really did understand why I had been panicking. I had this stupid idea that teachers don't mess up and I like it that she's human after all. Doing this course has been good for me – I enjoy coming to classes. I'm not yet the world's best writer but watch this space.

Critical thinking activity

» The teacher in this case study was able to empathise with Nosheen's predicament. What do you understand by the term empathy?

» Learners are sometimes described as having 'spiky' literacy or numeracy profiles. Research this term on the internet and apply it to your assessment of your learners.

In the previous chapter you saw how the features of professionalism are evident in the practical teaching of your subject specialism. Whatever your specialism happens to be, one extra you will want to throw in as part of the package, much as a car salesman might throw in a free warranty, is a commitment to support your learners in developing their literacy, numeracy and information and communication technology (ICT) skills. The chances are that you have learners who clearly struggle with one or more of these skills. You are also likely to have learners who appear to be confident but who are actually under-confident and anxious. Some, for example, will have a long history of poor numeracy skills that can compromise their learning in some subjects, and even today you may have learners who are nervous about using technology. Yet it is issues with literacy that you may well need to be most alert to because literacy affects just about any area of learning.

It is not always that easy for teachers to spot which learner is struggling because in order to survive with poor literacy skills you need to develop strategies that conceal the weakness. Lawrence (2000) suggests that there are signs for a teacher who is observant. In a classroom situation a learner might be reluctant to participate or they might make excuses for not completing homework. Learners with poor literacy skills often have low self-esteem so they might appear bored or boastful or blame others in order to boost their self-esteem. These strategies are understandable because poor literacy skills tend to be seen, more than either poor numeracy or ICT skills, as a reflection of a person's ability and intellect. For this reason, learners can become experts at camouflaging their difficulties.

> *For some the continual pressure of learning to cope with their literacy weakness can result in enormous stress... With regular failure in a skill that society values, people eventually lose confidence in themselves in general.*
>
> (Lawrence, 2000, Introduction)

Being good at communicating is sometimes thought of as having the ability to deliver a great lecture or produce a high standard of written handouts. Yet these skills, important though they are, form only a part of the picture. Good communication is probably even more about becoming aware of others and what they are experiencing. This is one of those statements that sounds easy in theory but is more difficult in practice. This is because each of us has a unique perspective of the world; we experience life, as it were, through the filters of our own unique pair of perceptual spectacles. Indeed, we see even very small things in our own individual way. You can test this yourself by thinking of a day of the week, any day, and asking yourself if you associate it with a particular colour. If you do, the chances are, if you were to ask a friend or colleague to do the same they would see the same day in a different colour. The anthropologist Clifford Geertz neatly sums up our unique view of the world when he says, 'man is an animal suspended in webs of significance that he himself has spun' (Geertz, 1973, p 5).

This means that on the whole we find it quite difficult to imagine things any other way but our own. If, for example, we find something like spelling or ICT easy we struggle to imagine what life must be like for someone who finds them difficult. Teaching is very much about crossing a metaphorical bridge to stand exactly where a learner is standing so that you can see things from their perspective. It is not only about gauging their thoughts and opinions, it's just as much an awareness of how they are feeling. This awareness, an ability to recognise and tune in to other people's emotions is a further aspect of emotional literacy that you looked at earlier in Chapter 3. It is often described as empathy, 'the drive to identify another person's emotions and thoughts and to respond to these with an appropriate emotion' (Simon Baron-Cohen, 2002, p 248).

The skill of showing empathy is something most of us are able to do instinctively. It happens, suggests the Dutch biologist Frans De Waal (2009), on a bodily level that we seldom think about. A child grazes a knee and we automatically, not only *say*, but *feel*, OUCH! Our stomach clenches and we experience a sharp intake of breath. Our body appears to share the experience of pain. It is this ability to feel that enables teachers to identify and support the learner who feels, whatever that feeling is, be it discomfort, resentment, puzzlement or anxiety. Empathy, suggests the educational and social psychologist Peter Sharp, is an essential communication skill, being

> *the basis of all interpersonal skills. An ability to read and tune in to other people's feelings is a core skill in letting people feel acknowledged and valued. It involves seeing the world through other people's eyes (and) responding appropriately to other people's moods, temperaments and motivations.*
>
> (Sharp, 2001, p 27)

Citing the work of Steiner (1977) and Goleman (1996), Sharp continues by suggesting that empathy enables us to manage conflict and is the basis for popularity, leadership and interpersonal effectiveness. It entails the ability to persuade others to work as individuals and in teams to achieve work-related goals. Given that the ability to empathise is something that most of us already possess, with such an excellent write-up, this powerful teaching skill is one that you will certainly want to nurture. Listening, observing and reflecting are the key skills needed, but it is curiosity, open-mindedness and the desire to know what makes others tick that are the catalysts.

There is one final point raised in this case study. Nosheen spoke of being confident that her fellow learners would not find out about her weakness in spelling and punctuation. This is important. Learners like Nosheen need to feel confident that their anxieties and concerns are taken seriously and treated with respect and confidentiality, and professional teachers will make sure they are.

Experiencing inclusion, co-operation and shared values

CASE STUDY

Matt

I began the A Level Economics course about six months ago. At first I always sat with my mates, even when we had to work in a group. Everyone in the class did the same. The girls all sat together – they didn't speak to us all that much. Then there was another group – they were all older and we'd sometimes talk to them but not a lot. And there were the four Chinese guys. They never said much. We'd all stay in our groups for breaks so we didn't really socialise with the others at all and I didn't know all that much about most of them, not even all their names. I didn't really think about it but I thought it worked OK.

Then we had a new teacher Carrie, and when she discovered how things were she asked us why we always worked in the same groups. At first no one answered and then Mick said, 'Well, I don't want to work with the Chinese guys. I don't think they know much because they never say anything so if I worked with them I'd have to do all the work, wouldn't I?' There were a few sniggers at this but Carrie said, 'How do you know this? Have you asked them anything or even spoken to them at all this week?' Mick had to admit that he hadn't said more than a couple of words to them since the beginning of term. Then Carrie asked us whether we thought there might be some good things about working together. A couple of the oldies said they thought we'd get to know each other a bit more and that was good, but the rest of us kept quiet.

At the start of the next class Carrie told us she had something she'd like us to work on. She said she wanted us to interview someone in the class we didn't know and then tell the rest of the class a bit about the person we'd interviewed. This idea got a mixed reception from us – some of the oldies were keen but most of us moaned about it. I decided to throw caution to the wind and do my interview on Liu, one of the Chinese guys. I thought it was going to be impossible to get her to say anything as she never speaks in class and if I couldn't find out anything about her it might mean I wouldn't have to do the talk. But she was really good at answering my questions although she told me that speaking in English is quite hard work and needed all her concentration. I was really surprised. Then we got talking about making the video links for our presentations on the budget and Liu said she can do it blindfolded and she'll help me with mine so that's ultra good. The Chinese guys aren't quiet at all; it is just part of their culture to be polite in class, but get them out of class and they are crazy.

The following week Carrie got us all to discuss our experience of doing the interviews and it was funny, everyone said it was good, they'd found out a lot of interesting stuff. Carrie said that this was a good opportunity to have a discussion about what sort of class atmosphere we wanted, like what was important to us. Everyone had lots to say. Mick said that he thought that it was important that we were polite and pleasant to each other, you know, not ignoring people but saying 'Hello' when you arrive. Someone said you can't like everyone in the class but we all agreed it's important to help each other because we're all good at different things. Karen, one of the oldies said that she was pleased that she now knew everyone by name and she thought it would be good if we thought about each other a bit more and helped each other. Carrie suggested we write these ideas down to make a sort of class mission statement.

Critical thinking activity

» *What do you think the learners gained from carrying out the interviews on each other?*

» *Do you agree or disagree with Carrie's decision to challenge Mick's comment about the Chinese learners? Give reasons.*

» *Think about a group of your learners. Do they form sub-groups? If so, is the composition of the groups by age, gender, race or something else? What activities might encourage these learners to form more open and co-operative relationships?*

Given an opportunity to complete open-ended course evaluations, learners will often make a point of saying how much they enjoyed the experience of working with other learners. That the experience of learning has much to do with the relationships of learning is a concept that has been well documented.

> *Learning is in its essence a fundamentally social phenomenon, reflecting our own deeply social nature as human beings.*
>
> (Wenger, 1998, p 3)

Teachers know that learners are influenced by the relationships they form as part of their learning and by the values, attitudes and behaviour of those around them. The explanation of why this happens lies in the fact that humans excel at synchrony, the unconscious instinct each of us possesses to mimic the sentiments of those around us. Take something obvious and visible like laughter; it's almost impossible not to laugh when surrounded by laughter. And we unconsciously and automatically absorb even the subtlest of sentiments evident in the situations in which we find ourselves. This process is described as follows:

> *Participation within a culture shapes individual disposition and physical behaviour in relation to their situation. Thus a person gets a feel for a situation which may look like the result of rational consideration, yet it is not based upon reasoning, but upon an unstated, usually unnoticed incorporation of culture which is simultaneously shaped through individual participation.*
>
> (Avis, Orr and Tummons, 2010, p 53)

Jenny Rogers puts this concept firmly into a teaching context with the following example.

> *Even with a group of apparently stable and self-possessed adults who contribute a good deal to an active discussion, their own moods of exhilaration, pleasure, boredom or irritation are invariably conveyed to a class, and that these reflections from their own personality are in some degree returned as mirror images in the way participants behave to them and to each other.*
>
> (Rogers, 2001, p 51)

Working co-operatively together, learning to give and take, helps to build respect and trust, a sound basis for the development of the shared values expressed in much educational theory. For example:

> *In order to have large numbers of values in common all the members of the group must have an equitable opportunity to receive and take from others.*
>
> (Dewey, 1916, p 84)

Learners are not necessarily active in seeking interaction with their fellow learners, often preferring to stay with those they know. This reluctance is understandable; people identify with those they know well and feel less comfortable with, and can even come to dislike those they see as different or unknown. We attach stereotypical labels easily and effortlessly to the lesser known; unchallenged, the assumptions implicit in these labels achieve acceptance. Mick's comment about the Chinese learners is a good example. So it may be necessary to actively encourage your learners to interact by providing opportunities for them to learn about each other and to share their experiences. And Rogers has a word of warning for teachers who focus overly on the teacher–learner relationship rather than the relationships between learners.

> *Don't make the common mistake of forgetting how important these (learner–learner) relationships are to learners because you are so preoccupied with the learners' relationship with you.*

> (Rogers, 2001, p 53)

It does seem to be the case that how individual learners think, feel and behave is shaped largely by what they experience through interaction with their teacher and their fellow learners. There is an opportunity here for you and your learners together to create a 'best' learning experience.

Features of a best learning experience

These case studies illustrate different facets of a best learning experience and reflect the distinctive brands offered by the teachers profiled. There are, however, a number of common features of a professional brand evident in the stories. It will be a brand:

- that promotes inclusion, harmony, co-operation, respect and trust;

- where learners are actively engaged in learning, are motivated, challenged, encouraged and supported;

- where learners' experiences and knowledge is valued by teachers;

- where learners can experience success and enjoy their learning.

A best learning experience scenario is far from guaranteed unless you take the bull by the horns, set the scene by example and initiate debate on core values. Rogers believes that teachers can and should be instrumental and active in determining the nature of their teaching groups.

> *Your influence is the most important single element in setting the style of a group: as great or even a greater influence on the whole occasion than the sum of all the other individuals.*

> (Rogers, 2001, p 51)

The task of establishing the values necessary for setting the style of a group that Rogers is talking about isn't necessarily problem free. No professional teacher would want to impose their own values on learners, and you are very likely to be conscious of the need to be sensitive to the different values and beliefs of your learners. Yet when introduced sensitively, with learners active and participative in the process, universal values such as equity and caring can be established within a group.

Critical thinking activity: identifying your teaching brand

» *What do you notice about the approach of the teachers in the case studies you have just looked at? Can you identify what these teachers have in common?*

» *Use the examples presented by the case studies to identify your teaching brand. What best experience do you want for your learners and what is your passion? What shared values do you feel are needed to achieve your vision?*

Conclusion

There is no off-the-peg version of a professional teaching brand: on the contrary it is unique, created and sustained by you and mediated by the relationships you have with your learners and they have with each other. Yet it will embody some core values and skills. Race and Pickford offer some features of excellent teaching, what the professional brand might look like from the learner's perspective, and Jenny Rogers gives a detailed description of the characteristics of good teaching. Here are the pared-down versions.

Excellent teaching is where:

- *learners look forward to learning;*

- *the teacher is approachable, caring, enthusiastic and sensitive;*

- *the teacher is liked, admired and respected by the learner.*

(Race and Pickford, 2007)

Effective teachers:

- *are warm, able to show approval and acceptance of learners and are able to weld the group together;*

- *generate and use learners' ideas and are skilled in spotting and resolving learner problems;*

- *are organised, enthusiastic, creative and resilient in the face of stress;*

- *stand up for what is right and encourage learners to push their boundaries;*

- *have presence and an ability to simplify the complex.*

(Rogers, 2001, p 75)

Chapter reflections

» *A professional teaching brand has a quality product, is well presented and offers learners a best learning experience.*

» *Teachers' personal values, beliefs and passions inform their professional practice.*

» *Teachers and learners together can establish and sustain a best learning experience.*

Taking it further

Lawrence, D (2000) *Building Self-Esteem with Adult Learners*. London: Sage.
This book by the psychologist Denis Lawrence is about enhancing self-esteem in the adult learner. He suggests that all learners have esteem needs and shows how you can recognise and respond to them.

Rogers, J (2001) *Adults Learning*. Buckingham: OU Press.
With lots of examples from her own experience of teaching, Jenny Rogers offers an accessible guide to teaching adults. This book includes chapters on what you need to know about your learners and understanding your teaching group.

References

Avis, J, Orr, K and Tummons, J (2010) Theorizing the Work-Based Learning of Teachers, in Avis, J, Fisher, R and Thompson, R (eds) *Teaching in Lifelong Learning*. Maidenhead: OU Press.

Baggini, J (2005) What Professionalism Means for Teachers Today, in *Education Review*, 18(2), Summer 2005. London: NUT.

Baron-Cohen, S (2002) The Extreme Male Brain Theory of Autism, in *Trends in Cognitive Sciences*, 6(6). Philadelphia: Elsevier.

De Waal, F (2009) *The Age of Empathy*. London: Souvenir Press Ltd.

Dewey, J (1938) *Experience and Education*. New York: Macmillan.

Geertz, C (1975) *The Interpretation of Cultures*. London: Hutchinson.

Hume, D (1969/1739–40) *A Treatise of Human Nature*. London: Penguin.

Humphreys, M and Hyland, T (2009) Theory, Practice and Performance in Teaching: Professionalism, Intuition and Jazz, in Avis, J, Fisher, R and Simmons, R (eds) *Issues in Post-Compulsory Education and Training*. Huddersfield: Huddersfield Press.

Lawrence, D (2000) *Building Self-Esteem with Adult Learners*. London: Sage.

Plato (2012) *The Phaedrus*. Michigan: Gale ECCO.

Race, P and Pickford, R (2007) *Making Teaching Work: Teaching Smarter in Post-Compulsory Education*. London: Sage.

Rogers, J (2001) *Adults Learning*. Buckingham: OU Press.

Sharp, P (2001) *Nurturing Emotional Literacy*. London: David Fulton Publishers Ltd.

Stott, N (2010) How Previous Experience Can Shape Our Teaching, in Wallace, S (eds) *The Lifelong Learning Sector Reflective Reader*. Exeter: Learning Matters.

Wenger, E (1998) *Communities of Practice: Learning, Meaning and Identity*. Cambridge: Cambridge University Press.

7 The professional club: a membership guide

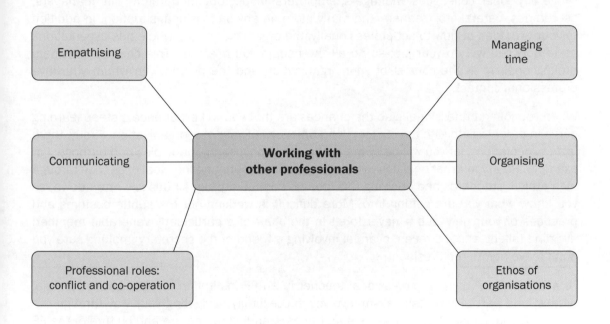

Chapter aims

This chapter will help you to:

- understand the nature and culture of the FE sector and of your organisation;

- understand how people function professionally in organisations and resolve issues of role conflict;

- identify and analyse the professional skills needed to work effectively with colleagues and others.

Introduction

So far this book has concentrated predominantly on professionalism in the context of your relationship to learners. But this only tells part of the story because you do not operate in isolation from others; you work in an organisational setting, with key relationships with a wide range of people: colleagues, managers, employers, inspectors, moderators, site managers, secretaries, caretakers, cleaners and many more. In any professional situation, in addition to your own idea of how to act professionally, the organisation as a whole has expectations as to how you will do your job; so do all the people you relate to. This chapter considers professionalism in the context of your organisation and the people with whom you have professional contact.

When you join a professional club the chances are that you will experience a steep learning curve in order to fit in with the customs and practices of your new organisation. Firstly, there is an expectation that you will be aware of the club's philosophy, principles and purpose. For example, Rotary International has a key objective of encouraging the ideal of service through high ethical standards and applying this ideal to community life. All this is written down, so you know what you are getting into. More difficult is working out the subtle customs and practices of your new club – never to sit in the chair of a particularly venerable member; avoiding talking about a recent scandal involving a friend of the secretary; making sure you don't leave before the President.

To a large extent being a professional teacher in an FE institution has the same potential pitfalls, and part of professionalism involves successfully navigating your way through the organisational jungle. This chapter is about understanding the nature and culture of the FE sector and of your own organisation. This understanding forms the basis of a discussion on how you as a professional teacher can operate effectively in your working environment.

Nature and culture of FE organisations

Diversity implies that every organisation is different, with its own unique character and culture. It should be possible, however, to use theoretical models to gain an insight into the nature of your organisation so that you may be able to work more effectively with your colleagues and to give a more professional service to your learners. Two renowned organisational behaviour and management specialists, Charles Handy (1993) and Peter Senge (2006), have contributed important insights concerning the ethos of organisations and the effects of this ethos on the professionals who work within it.

Handy's contribution is a classic identification and analysis of different organisational cultures. He identified four main cultures that he named role, task, person and power. Here are the main features of each culture.

*   *Role culture* – a rigid system emphasising the importance of professional roles, with detailed job descriptions and written procedures. In this culture there is a strong tendency towards impersonality, with individuals seeming to be less important than the posts they occupy.

*   *Task culture* – a more flexible culture, with emphasis given to networks, task groups and personal expertise. It is characterised by specialist teams that are formed for specific high-priority tasks and which disperse when the task is completed.

*   *Person culture* – a culture that gives primacy to expert professionals and to whom the organisation is subordinate, primarily providing facilities to support these experts. This culture is often found in small professional organisations such as law firms or medical practices.

*   *Power culture* – a competitive culture with power wielded by key individuals, often exercising their influence through charisma or control of resources. It is characterised by a competitive atmosphere in which individuals are primarily judged by results.

Handy was not writing about FE colleges, but was concerned with commercial profit-making enterprises. Since that time FE organisations have, as we have seen, become far more business oriented, and Handy's views are probably more apposite today than they were in 1993. He recognised that organisations do not fall neatly into one culture or another but often exhibit features of several. He also realised that events, such as the appointment of a new managing director, could change the abiding culture. He did believe, however, that it was possible to analyse an organisation at a given point in time and identify a tendency towards one culture or another.

Another model you might find useful in understanding your own organisation is that developed by Peter Senge. He coined the term 'learning organisation' to describe an organisation that facilitates the professional development of its staff and is a community to which staff feel committed. There are some specific features of learning organisations that have particular relevance to the professional role of FE teachers: personal mastery, shared vision and team learning.

*   *Personal mastery* describes a high level of individual professional commitment to the process of learning, and an organisational culture that encourages and demonstrates this commitment through its policies.

*   *Shared vision* is owned by all members of the organisation rather than imposed from above. It is important in motivating staff, creating a common identity and commitment to learning.

*   *Team learning* encourages staff to develop professionally more quickly and improves the problem-solving capacity of the organisation through better access to knowledge

and expertise. Learning organisations have structures that encourage team learning, open dialogue and discussion.

Like Handy, Peter Senge had commercial enterprises in mind when he described a learning organisation. However, the development of a more market-oriented FE sector in recent years has, if anything, increased the relevance of Senge's work. If your organisation has a vision that is shared among all staff and facilitates personal mastery and team learning, this may well make the development of your own professionalism that much easier.

Critical thinking activity: analysing your organisation

» *Identify any features of Handy's four cultures that are evident in your organisation. What is the dominant culture and what are the consequences of this in fulfilling your professional role?*

» *To what extent does your organisation fulfill Senge's three criteria of learning organisations detailed above?*

Working in a professional organisation: conflict and co-operation

Understanding the culture and ethos of your organisation is a good basis for considering how you as a professional can work effectively with colleagues and others, for your own self-esteem and ultimately for the benefit of your learners. The establishment of effective relationships with others in turn depends on an understanding of how people function in organisations.

You may remember that the concept of professional identity was discussed in Chapter 3. This is the set of beliefs, attitudes and understandings about your work that you bring with you when you take up an appointment in FE. Once you are there this identity becomes an identity in action; in simple terms you start playing your professional role. You are also surrounded by people who are acting out their own roles, raising the possibility of conflict and misunderstanding. It is time to have a closer look at roles and their relevance to working professionally in an FE organisation.

Much of our understanding of roles is based on the work of a Canadian sociologist, Erving Goffman (1990), who used the imagery of the theatre as a metaphor to analyse role playing in action. Goffman invites us to see life like a theatrical performance where the actors (the people you interact with) are on stage in front of an audience (that is, everyone who sees what you are doing). We play roles all the time: parent, customer, friend, partner and many others as well as the professional role of teacher.

Roles are all about expectations – both your expectations of how you should behave and the expectations of people you are working with, known as your role set. You are expected to dress in a certain way, to speak in a certain way, to act in a certain way depending on the role you are playing. For example, you will have a clear idea of how you should dress for a job interview and the people interviewing you will also have expectations about your appearance. Problems arise when people's expectations differ. So we come to role conflict.

Role conflict takes two forms. Firstly, there is conflict between roles when you are forced to choose between two different and incompatible roles at the same time. For example, if you are offered a better job that would mean moving to another part of the country and disrupting your children's education at a critical time, there is potential conflict between your professional role and your role of being a good parent. Secondly, there is conflict within a role when your interpretation of your role differs from how others see it. The following case study illustrates this point.

CASE STUDY

Mohsin's new job

Mohsin has just taken up a new appointment teaching Communication Studies within the Business and Management school at a large FE college and is having trouble settling in. Here is an extract from the reflective journal that he keeps as part of his CPD programme.

I'm not sure that I'll ever be comfortable in this job; it's so different to my last job. I used to teach GCSE to some pretty rough lads, and the whole ethos of the place was relaxed and democratic. All the staff dressed casually – jeans and T-shirts and so on; my boss sat in the same staffroom and was more of a friend than a line manager; we often decided quite important things over a cup of coffee when the whole team got together at the end of the day and it worked fine. I was very happy and think that as a team we were all really professional and got good results.

It's very different here. For a start, everything is far more formal; dress is jacket and tie, I rarely see my boss because she sits in a separate office and you feel you have to book an appointment just to have a chat. We have meetings in which formal minutes are taken, and decisions come down from high by e-mail. Quite autocratic and it feels stifling.

I don't really know what to do. Is it professional to change my style to conform and feel that I am acting a part that seems artificial? Or should I come to work and do my job in the more informal way I have been used to and which suits my personal style, and be seen by everyone I work with as some sort of oddball who won't conform?

Critical thinking activity

» *Is it more professional for Mohsin to conform to the ethos of his new working environment or should he continue to behave as he did in his previous college? Is there room for compromise? Give reasons for your answer.*

If Mohsin can resolve his problems of relating to his new group of colleagues there are potentially great rewards of working within a group of people who share a profession. Most organisations comprise many small groups or teams that share information and experiences so that they learn from each other, and have a good opportunity to develop personally and professionally. The anthropologist Etienne Wenger (1998) believed that learning takes place wherever people get together and relate to one another. He identified such groups as 'communities of practice' and defined three elements that characterise them.

1. *Mutual engagement*: In any group or community, members start to build collaborative relationships, which gradually reinforce the identity of the group as a social entity.

2. *Joint enterprise*: This is the common understanding that develops with time and experience and which binds the group together.

3. *Shared repertoire*: This represents the shared customs and behaviours of the group that develop in time and reinforce the community's motivation and unique character.

Wenger was primarily thinking of commercial enterprises when he published his work on communities of practice. For example, he described the experience of Xerox service representatives who began exchanging tips and hints over informal meetings during lunch breaks. Eventually Xerox management incorporated these tips and they were subsequently shared across the Xerox global network.

This clearly echoes Peter Senge's ideas about team learning in learning organisations. It is not difficult to see how both concepts can be applied to FE professionals. If you belong to an effective team or community of practice, perhaps based round your staffroom colleagues or people who share your enthusiasm for your subject area, this is clearly beneficial for your own professionalism and your learners.

Critical thinking activity: role conflict and communities of practice

»   *Consider your own working environment. What instances of role conflict have you experienced and how have you resolved them?*

»   *What communities of practice do you belong to? To what extent and in what ways do these groups encourage your own learning and professional development?*

Working with colleagues: professional skills

You may remember the story of Mel in Chapter 3, who had problems in co-operating with her colleagues. This was in the context of examining Mel's values and beliefs, but there are other implications for her professional practice. The professional skills of teaching, such as effective communication, empathy, time management, organising and administrative skills are equally important in dealing with colleagues and others as they are with learners.

Communicating with colleagues and others

Channels of communication

Organisations have a variety of communication styles and processes, but there are some common features. One such feature is the distinction between formal and informal communications. Formal systems are the official communication channels in an organisation. Typically these channels will involve written communications, such as staff handbooks, management directives, letters and so on. They will also include records of meetings, interviews, appraisals and other formal face-to-face discussions. Informal systems include the routine discussions, telephone conversations, notes left on desks and face-to-face chats between colleagues, which occur throughout every working day. They seldom form part of the official communication records that end up on official files, but they constitute a considerable part of the overall communication that takes place in an organisation's daily life.

On top of this, you need to be aware of grapevines. Information doesn't always flow smoothly through these formal and informal channels and this is where grapevines appear and flourish. You can see grapevines in action in coffee-room chats, passing the time at the photocopying machine, sharing the latest gossip as you meet a colleague in the corridor. There is always a grapevine in an organisation. It seems that where communication in an organisation does not function effectively, the grapevine will prosper.

Problems of communication with colleagues

Even if your organisation has excellent communication systems, things will occasionally go wrong and test your professionalism. Sometimes messages get distorted, sometimes they go astray or get lost. When these problems arise, it can be potentially damaging for you and your learners, because you may pass on incorrect information or not be aware of information that they need. Govinda Parr, a part-time lecturer teaching Computing at an adult education centre suffered in this way.

CASE STUDY

'Nobody ever tells you anything in this place!'

Govinda teaches Microsoft Office to two groups of adult learners each for three hours per week. One group of 20 learners attends on Monday evenings, the other class of 15 comes on Wednesday evenings. She is not happy, as this journal entry illustrates.

I'm royally fed up. I seem to be constantly being messed about, never told anything in time and often it's wrong anyway. Yesterday was a good example. At 3 o'clock in the afternoon I get a message from Ruth, the centre secretary, to ask why I wasn't at the centre staff meeting that James, the centre manager, had arranged to talk about problems with some of the computer suites. I said that I didn't know about the meeting, only to be told that she (Ruth) had put a message in my pigeonhole and also sent an e-mail about it.

I dashed into the centre, just in time to catch the end of the meeting and to learn that my computer room was going to be out of action for two days because of a wiring problem and my class would have to make do with Room 6, which only has twelve serviceable PCs. So now I have less than two hours to re-cast tonight's lesson for 20 students and only 12 available machines. I think my groups are getting a raw deal, and it makes me look unprofessional and incompetent.

What really makes me angry is that the rewiring and room change had been scheduled over a week ago. If I'd known in time I could have arranged for some of my Monday crowd to come on Wednesday this week. As it was, the message was put in my pigeonhole last

Thursday, after I'd finished teaching for the week, and the e-mail message went to George Parr, who teaches Maths! I need to sort things out with Ruth, as this isn't the first time she's messed up.

Critical thinking activity

» *What actions could be taken to improve communication in the centre and avoid situations like this arising in future? What could Govinda have done to avoid the problem of not being informed about the meeting and the room change?*

Clearly there are communication problems at this centre. Just because messages are sent, it does not mean they have been received. In this case e-mail addresses are not accurate, no acknowledgement of receipt of messages is required, the consequences of changing rooms at such short notice have not been considered and there is a problem with keeping part-time staff informed in good time when they are only at work for a couple of days a week. Ruth and James have a few questions to answer.

As for Govinda, she's been put in a difficult position because she didn't receive a message on time. The important thing is to avoid a similar situation arising in future, and there are some things she could do. These include confirming with Ruth and James when she will be out of contact, when she will be in the centre next and how they can leave messages. This could perhaps be done by e-mail, memo, a face-to-face chat or a combination of these. She will need to 'sort things out' in a professional way.

It is clear from the tone of Govinda's writing that she is not in a mood which is kindly disposed towards Ruth. There is a danger here that her animosity will affect the way she responds and she will not obtain the outcome that she wants. You do not have the luxury of choosing the people you work with, and one of the features of good professional behaviour is to manage situations where colleagues do not get on with each other. Sir David Brailsford, the manager of the Sky cycling team that has produced two Tour de France winners put this succinctly in the context of the personal relationship between Bradley Wiggins and Chris Froome. He is quoted as saying that he didn't care if people liked each other or not as long as they understood the difference between personal and professional behaviour and were 100 per cent committed to the goal. Govinda is not going to try to win the Tour de France, but she nevertheless has a goal that should be shared by all her colleagues: to give the best possible professional service to her learners.

Govinda's story illustrates that it's a lot easier to communicate with people you like, and not so easy to communicate with those who are antagonistic towards you. This is important because your professional behaviour in relating to your colleagues is to a large extent expressed in how you communicate with them, in the way you speak and the tone of your writing and so forth. Paradoxically, communicating in a professional manner makes dealing with someone you don't like a bit easier. Professionalism in this context means communicating effectively no matter who you are communicating with. The aim is to be clear, dispassionate and objective, and to avoid being influenced by the sort of emotional antagonism that Govinda's mood may well reflect. Patrick's story illustrates this.

CASE STUDY

Patrick and Richard

Patrick is a newly appointed training officer at a large engineering firm and he has responsibility for running Health and Safety courses in the company's training centre. Richard is a more experienced training officer at the same firm. Although there is no open animosity between them, Patrick has the suspicion that Richard is resentful because Patrick was appointed in preference to Richard's wife who also applied for the job. One Tuesday morning the following e-mail appears in Patrick's inbox.

To: Patrick Harvey

From: Richard Browning

Subject: Training suite issues

Patrick

I am concerned about the way you are using the training room. This morning I found all the furniture had been moved to the side and I had to spend ten minutes rearranging it before my supervisory studies group arrived. This is not the first time this situation has occurred and I think it shows an unprofessional approach for a training officer in this company. Please ensure that in future you replace the desks and chairs in the configuration that you found them. In the event of any repetition I will be compelled to report the matter formally to the Training Manager.

Richard

Patrick's first reaction to this message was one of righteous anger. He took exception to the aggressive tone of the e-mail and felt that, as he had seen Richard in the staffroom during yesterday's lunch break, the complaint could have been dealt with over a coffee and chat. To add insult to injury, Patrick had left the room exactly as he had found it. In fact, the cleaners had stacked the furniture against the wall when they cleaned the room over the weekend and not replaced it. He was particularly incensed at being called unprofessional, and resented the implied threat to initiate a formal complaint to their line manager. Patrick drafted a strongly worded reply explaining why the furniture had been left at the sides of the room, underscoring his resentment at being called unprofessional and copying the email to the training manager.

Critical thinking activity

» *Should Patrick press the 'send' button? If so, what would be the likely consequences? Can you think of a more effective way of responding?*

Patrick's draft e-mail has all the hallmarks of an emotional reaction to Richard's brusque complaint about finding an unprepared training room just before his class was due. Clearly, Richard was venting his frustration on the most vulnerable target – Patrick, the new boy who got the job his wife applied for. It would clearly have been better – and more professional – for Richard to wait until he had calmed down and then to talk to Patrick informally. In this way, he would have avoided upsetting Patrick and learned the background to the furniture configuration.

By the same token, if Patrick sends an aggressive and emotive reply while he is still upset, the chances are that the confrontation will escalate and drag in their line manager needlessly. Patrick and Richard will have to work together in future, and both can do without the lingering antagonism of a petty dispute. So there is probably an advantage for Patrick not to press the 'send' button but instead to ask Richard if they could have a chat about the problem over a cup of coffee.

There is one final point in this case study; Patrick has good reason to feel resentful about the personal comment on his lack of professionalism and he would be fully justified in letting Richard know how he feels. The important thing is to raise the issue in a non-confrontational way, to respond objectively and avoid personal criticism. And there is always recourse to take the issue to his line manager if it cannot be solved amicably.

Communication in groups

One specific arena of communication that is a little more complex is group communication, most usually seen in the numerous meetings that professional teachers find themselves attending as part of the daily routine. You may well have a love–hate relationship with meetings; tedious and time consuming on the one hand, but a necessary evil to get things done on the other. The communication process is more complex in this context because groups tend to develop an identity of their own in which individual members are just a part, and because group members adopt specific roles in relating to other members; some are quiet, some extravert, some conciliatory, some confrontational.

The tendency to adopt one specific role in a group depends on several factors; personality, group size, time pressures and so on. Research has indicated that the most effective groups tend to have a diverse composition to which members contribute different strengths and styles. Maurice Belbin (1993) made this point and identified nine different roles in group transactions. He gave names to these roles like co-ordinator, implementer, finisher and plant. As part of your professional practice in communicating with groups of colleagues, there is some advantage in knowing the roles that you prefer to enact in meetings.

Critical thinking activity: working in groups

» *Using internet and library sources, investigate Belbin's work on group roles. Which of his categories is most appropriate to you? In what way does this affect your professional practice?*

Empathy

We saw earlier that empathy, the ability to see things from another's point of view and to accept that they may have a different but valid viewpoint, is a key professional skill in your relationship with learners. It is an equally important skill in dealing with colleagues and others in your role set.

Difficulties can occur when you see others in terms of the job they do, the professional role they are playing, rather than as individuals. When Simon is sitting in your staffroom drinking coffee, will you talk to him in the same way if he is the Vice Principal as you would if he were the department cleaner? You may come across a trace of academic arrogance in your organisation where some academic staff see themselves as key high-status figures and others – such as technicians, catering or clerical staff – are seen as being employed merely to provide support to them. If this attitude is reflected in behaviour that does not value colleagues for themselves but merely sees them as holders of a low-status position, problems will arise.

CASE STUDY

Jacob's ladder

Jacob is a maintenance technician whose job is to look after an annex and workshop for the construction crafts school at an FE college. He has been in the post for fifteen years and takes considerable pride in ensuring that the building is maintained to a high standard. He has had a difficult conversation with Mike, the newly appointed Head of Construction, and shares his thoughts with Francesca, the Principal's PA, who is an old friend and neighbour.

This new bloke Mike is causing all sorts of grief. Just because he's the head of school and got a degree he seems to think we should all bow and scrape to him. This morning he stormed into the office and gave me a right earful about a set of ladders he'd asked me to shift because they were blocking the entrance to the workshop. I tried to explain that I had moved them yesterday but Jim's brickwork class must have used them this morning and left them there again, but he just wouldn't listen. He said the techies at his old college would never have tolerated such a hazard to safety and that it showed a sloppy attitude that needed to improve.

I haven't felt so humiliated since I started to work here. What made it worse was that a couple of students and my gofer Tony were in the office listening to him ranting on, and I nearly lost my rag. Fortunately Tony looked at me and I bit my lip. Afterwards he said he'd heard Mike yelling at his secretary about some mail that had not been filed and made her cry. I just wish Eric were still head of school. He could be hard but always treated you fairly. He took an interest in what you were doing and often came into the office to chat and say thanks if I'd done something a bit extra. You felt that you were treated like a person doing something worthwhile, not some sort of minion whose opinion didn't matter. I tell you, there won't be many extra favours done for this guy unless he changes a bit smartish!

Critical thinking activity

» *How would you describe Mike's behaviour in terms of his professionalism? What are the likely consequences of this incident?*

You can probably identify clear examples of unprofessional behaviour in this case study. Criticising a subordinate in front of other colleagues, coming to conclusions before hearing the entire story, communicating in an aggressively emotive way are just a few instances. But the main criticism of Mike's professionalism stems from his lack of empathy as revealed by the story. He feels superior because of his appointment and does not value the contribution of his staff, and this attitude is obvious to them.

As for consequences, the most likely is a distinct lack of co-operation from the staff on the receiving end of his authoritarian approach. Respect is something that is earned, not automatically granted by virtue of being a boss. Morale in the school is likely to suffer, with professional motivation put under severe stress. In the final analysis it is the learners who are likely to suffer if they are being taught by teachers who are unhappy and resentful.

As an afterthought, you might speculate on the chances of this story eventually reaching the ears of the Principal in some form or other. Principals have been known to use their PA as a source to keep in touch with what is going on in their college, and in this story there is some 'grapevine potential' for this to happen.

Time management, organising and administrative skills

Teaching in FE is a pressure job. There are countless demands placed on you in the routine of a normal working day in addition to teaching your learners: meetings, memos, phone calls, e-mails, colleagues demanding your attention, directives from your line manager to name but a few. Sometimes these can be difficult to manage, as the following case study illustrates.

CASE STUDY

If I only had time...

Jenny is an outstanding teacher who is finding it difficult to cope with the demands of her job as a teacher in the Social Studies section of a small FE college. She confides in a friend after a particularly difficult day.

Fresh start Monday – I was really looking forward to today. Although I had to finish a tedious report to David, my line manager, for a meeting with him at 2 o'clock, I had two hours teaching my favourite BTEC class to start the day and another two hours teaching the C & G level 3 group from 3 o'clock. I reckoned I could easily get the report done in the middle of the day. Chance would be a fine thing!

The first problem came when Raju asked to see me at the end of the BTEC class. He's a good learner but very quiet and doesn't contribute much. It transpires that his mum is very ill and he thinks he may have to leave the course. I'd really be sorry to lose him and eventually arranged for him to have a chat with Student Services, but it took ages for him to tell me all this – he's so shy and was on the verge of tears a few times.

So when I got back to the office I found a phone message on my desk marked urgent, dozens of e-mails in my inbox, a pile of letters and Jim the technician asking how I wanted the room set up for Wednesday's class. I sorted him out first, but had to go over to the room to show him exactly what I wanted – another 20 minutes gone and not even a chance for a coffee.

When I got back to my desk, I started on David's report when Diana from the local Social Services office arrived to discuss what I wanted her to do when she comes to talk to the BTEC group next week. She said she'd phoned earlier this morning to confirm it was OK unless I rang back. So that was the urgent phone call! Anyway we had a good chat, although it was interrupted by a phone call from the C & G external verifier about some projects I'd sent him as a sample of my students' work. Diana kept glancing at her watch, but at least we sorted out details of her visit.

By now it's 1.00 pm – no lunch yet and I have only just started on the report. A quick take-away sandwich at my desk and on with this boring report. Then at 1.45 the marketing manager phoned asking me if I'd seen her e-mail about next year's brochure. Had to put her off and say I'd ring back later. Just finished the report in time, but then took five minutes to find the appendices in the chaos of my desk. So a bit late for the meeting, but at least managed to get back to the classroom for the 3 o'clock class – heaven!

I love teaching. The classes are great and it's a delight to be helping others learn. But by the end of the day I'm completely exhausted. All the admin and hassle is getting me down, and if anything it looks like it's going to get worse as the term goes on. I'm not sure I can cope for much longer.

Critical thinking activity

» What strategies could Jenny adopt to avoid the problems she has experienced in this study? Compare your responses to the comments below

You probably feel some sympathy with Jenny's problem. Teaching can be an exhausting business at the best of times and everyone gets tired, particularly towards the end of a difficult day or towards the end of term. Added to this, there is no doubt that in the last 20 years the administrative demands on academic staff have dramatically increased. Audits, Ofsted inspections, evaluation processes and the need to demonstrate accountability have all contributed to this trend, and it is easy to see why Jenny feels so stressed and overburdened.

That is not to say that all of this stress is inevitable. Jenny is clearly not in control of her working day and spends much of her time firefighting – reacting to other people's issues and never finding time to pursue her own agenda. Thus her filing system is disorganised, e-mails do not get read or actioned promptly, she is constantly dealing with interruptions, is late for her appointment and does not have time to do anything properly. If this leads to a reputation for unreliability among her colleagues, even being an outstanding teacher will not prevent her from being seen as unprofessional to some extent.

The root of her problem is time management: she just does not have enough time to do her job effectively. If she improved her time management skills it would create the opportunity to be better organised and to manage her administrative tasks better. In other words she would operate more professionally.

Fortunately, time management is a skill that can be learned, and there are several well-known techniques that Jenny could use. These techniques differ in detail but they are based on similar methodologies. The main elements are as follows.

- *Make a list of tasks you need to do.* Such lists can vary between long-term goals that can take years to complete down to tasks that you want to finish in a day. Jenny does not seem to have a list but at least she has identified one key task she must do – write the report to her line manager.

- *Prioritise the tasks on your list.* A common approach is to divide them into groups: urgent, important, not urgent and not important tasks. You can then classify them under four headings:

    1. Tasks that are urgent and important – the highest priority, to be done first with enough time allocated for completion. Jenny's report to her line manager falls into this category.

    2. Tasks that are important but not urgent – the next priority level, to have time allocated, but not necessarily to be done immediately. There may be some of these tasks in Jenny's e-mails, but she does not have time to look at them.

    3. Tasks that are urgent but not important – could be done quickly if there is nothing urgent and important that needs to be done first. Diana's phone call falls into this group.

    4. Tasks that are neither urgent nor important – lowest priority. To be done at some convenient time, preferably before the task becomes urgent!

- *Scheduling your time.* This ensures that urgent tasks are done in time and that enough time is allocated to do important tasks properly. It involves identifying the time you have available, blocking in the 'important and urgent' tasks in your schedule first and continuing blocking in tasks as you go down your priority list. In the case study Jenny really needs to give a block of priority time to get her report done before 2pm. Allow contingency time to take account of unpredictable situations. If you run out of time, either postpone the lower priority tasks for the next schedule or try to negotiate an extension of time for some tasks.

- *Completing your tasks.* Even if you have listed, prioritised and scheduled your tasks, actually putting this plan into action has numerous pitfalls. However, a disciplined approach can work wonders in avoiding them.

- *Interruptions.* If you are engaged in your highest priority task, by definition you should avoid interruption. You do not have to answer the phone; ignore it, use voice mail, go into another room. The external verifier's phone call could have been put on voice mail and dealt with later. You do not have to deal with other people's problems such as Jim's immediately. Publicise your 'available' and 'not available' time and put a 'Do Not Disturb' sign on the door. Find a quiet room to work in. You certainly do not have to be distracted by incoming e-mails; keep your e-mail programme closed, check your inbox at set times of the day that do not interfere with important or urgent tasks.

- *Lost documents.* You need an organised filing system for both paper and electronic documents. Time spent initially naming and organising folders in a consistent manner that suits your personal style is time well spent. One of your important regular tasks, maybe daily or perhaps weekly, should be to get your filing up to date. This might have avoided Jenny's problems with the mislaid appendices to her report.

- *Procrastination.* You will doubtless have jobs you dislike doing, and sometimes yield to the temptation to postpone them and do something more pleasant. This may be because the task is tedious or threatens to overwhelm you. However, if the task is important and/or urgent, procrastination will only lead to greater difficulty. Jenny is clearly less than enthusiastic about her report, but her reluctance to tackle it and willingness to be distracted only made matters worse. The solution lies in self-motivation. Intrinsically, this could be pride in your professionalism. Extrinsically, one technique to avoid procrastination might be to think about the unpleasant consequences of inaction; another could be to promise yourself a reward when the task is done. Either way, if you stick to the discipline imposed by your task priorities, you should be able to solve the problem.

Critical thinking activity: time management

» *Research the time management techniques of ABC analysis, Pareto analysis, the Eisenhower method and the POSEC method. Consider which of these techniques might be appropriate for your own professional practice.*

Conclusion: working with colleagues and others

This chapter has argued that it is not sufficient for you to develop a high standard of professional teaching skills. Additionally, professionalism requires you to understand how your organisation works and how to work effectively with colleagues and others in your role set. Fortunately there is considerable overlap between the two professional identities of teacher and member of an academic community. Professional skills such as empathy, effective communication and time management are equally important professional attributes in the staffroom as in the classroom.

Chapter reflections

» *FE institutions have distinct and individual cultures.*

» *Your organisation can be analysed in terms of its dominant culture and its characteristics as a learning organisation.*

» *Management of role conflict is an important factor in establishing effective working relationships with colleagues and others in your role set.*

» *Effective communication, empathy, time management, organising and administrative skills are key professional skills in dealing with people in your role set.*

Taking it further

Appleyard, N and Appleyard, K (2010) *Communicating with Learners*. Exeter: Learning Matters.
This book contains a section (Chapters 9 and 10) on the nature of communicating in organisations and with colleagues.

Armitage, A, Bryant, R, Dunnill, R, Flanagan, K, Hayes, D, Hudson, A, Kent, J, Lawes, S and Renwick, M (2007) *Teaching and Training in Post-Compulsory Education*. Maidenhead: McGraw Hill.
The section of this book entitled *Working in the LLS* covers many of the issues and strategies of working effectively with colleagues in an FE institution.

Avis, J, Fisher, R and Simmons, R (2009) *Issues in Post-Compulsory Education and Training: Critical Perspectives*. Huddersfield: University of Huddersfield Press.
Chapter 3 covers the concept of communities of practice.

Morgenstern, J (2004) *Time Management from the Inside Out*. New York: Owl Books.
This is an authoritative guide to time management techniques.

References

Belbin, M (1993) *Team Roles at Work*. Oxford: Butterworth-Heinemann.
Goffman, E (1990) *The Presentation of Self in Everyday Life*. London: Penguin.
Handy, C (1993) *Understanding Organisations*. London: Penguin.
Senge, P (2006) *The Fifth Discipline: The Art and Practice of the Learning Organisation*. London: Random House.
Wenger, E (1998) *Communities of Practice*. New York: Cambridge University Press.

Websites

www.mindtools.com (last accessed 6 February 2014)

8 Thinking matters: from hindsight to fortune telling

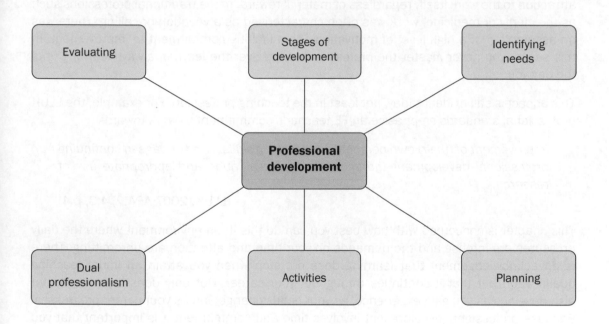

Chapter aims

This chapter will help you to:

- understand the stages of professional development;

- recognise the dual nature of being a professional teacher and a subject specialist;

- identify your own professional development needs;

- plan your professional development;

- identify appropriate development activities to meet your needs;

- use the techniques of critical reflection to evaluate your professional development.

Introduction

One of the key features of professionalism discussed in Chapter 2 was the aspect of an attraction to the work itself, regardless of material reward. In the traditional professions such as the clergy or medicine, work was often characterised as a vocation or calling. There was an assumption of a high level of motivation and a lifelong commitment to improvement. In this sense, you never master the profession but are ever the learner, always learning until the day you retire.

This aspect is still evident today, not least in the teaching profession. For example, the LLUK professional standards emphasise an FE teacher's commitment to work towards

> *improvement of (their) own personal and teaching skills... and engage in continuing professional development through reflection, evaluation and appropriate use of research.*
>
> (LLUK, 2007 AP4.2, 4.3, p 4)

This chapter is concerned with how best you can do this in an environment where the daily pressures are intense and the demands on your time and attention are unremitting. There is an acknowledgement that learning does not stop when you attain an initial teaching qualification but that it continues throughout your career. Not only does it continue, but also develops as you gain experience, as your needs change and as your career progresses. Because professional development involves time and commitment it is important that you can use your previous experience to work out how you want to develop professionally in the future – hence from hindsight to fortune telling.

The nature of continuing professional development (CPD)

The nature of your CPD depends to a significant degree on the stage you have reached in your career, and there are several models that illustrate this.

Stuart and Hugh Dreyfus (1980) analysed professional expertise in occupations such as senior managers and airline pilots, and described a five-stage progression of skill acquisition from novice to expert as primarily dependent on learning from experience. Thus the novice starts with a rigid adherence to rules and progresses through advanced beginner, competence and proficiency stages to expert status where behaviour and performance become almost intuitive. What is notable about this model is the emphasis on practical experience with only occasional mention of theoretical learning as a component of professional development. This can be seen as a reaction to the content of many traditional training courses that included a high proportion of theoretical content regardless of how much of this was ever used in practice.

Another model of development of professional competence was that of Michael Eraut (1994) who saw professional skills being acquired by a combination of learning from books, learning from people and learning from personal experience. He saw the importance of how theory gets interpreted in practice and how people form theoretical generalisations from their practical experience. The emphasis here is on a mixture of formal and informal learning, with professionals increasingly able to identify and choose the most appropriate method as their experience increases.

Susan Wallace describes a similar model of professional development, citing an article by Anthony Gregorc who envisaged a four-stage process that he called becoming, growing, maturing and fully functional.

> *The development needs he identifies for the first stage, 'Becoming' – focusing on the use of methods and resources and the skills of planning – might be referred to as a survival kit for teachers... In the next phase, 'Growing', the teacher's development needs are for consolidation and expansion of these skills and strategies. The third phase, which Gregorc labels 'Maturing', involves strong personal commitment, increased willingness to experiment and an ability to tolerate ambiguity... (In) the final 'Fully functioning' phase the teacher has developed a high level of self-direction and astute skills of self-evaluation based on self-referenced norms. Here the teacher's needs move definitively into the area of self-development and will lead the teacher to seek continuing opportunities for personal and professional growth.*
> (Wallace, 2007, p 76)

Critical thinking activity: the nature of professional development

» *To what extent do you feel that an understanding of theory is important in professional development?*

» *Using the internet and library resources, research in more detail the concept of stages in professional development. Identify the current stage of development in your own professional career.*

Factors affecting your CPD

Several factors influence your CPD. These include the stage you have reached in your career, the opportunities provided by your organisation, your prospects and your aspirations. Additionally, there is the political and economic context of contemporary FE.

After years of benign neglect, in which CPD was often a lottery dependent on where you worked and who you worked for, successive governments have sought to introduce CPD as an essential part of the policy of professionalising the FE sector. Jeanne Hitching cites David Blunkett's persuasive justification of this policy as follows:

> *Nobody expects a doctor, accountant or lawyer to rely for decades solely on the knowledge, understanding and approach which was available at the time when they began their career. Good professionals are engaged in a journey of self-improvement, always ready to reflect on their own practice in the light of other approaches and contribute to the development of others by sharing their best practice and insights.*

(Hitching, 2008, p ix)

As you saw in Chapter 2, the 2007 regulations included a requirement that FE teachers, in order to maintain their licence to practise, needed to undertake and evidence at least 30 hours of CPD in any one year. QTLS status therefore demonstrated a teacher's commitment to continue to develop the skills and knowledge acquired while training to be a teacher. The IfL, in addition to issuing a licence to practise and generally fulfilling the roles traditionally undertaken by other professional bodies, was given the task of managing the CPD process nationally. The pendulum had swung from one extreme to the other. From a system where professional development was spasmodic and fragmented, FE teachers suddenly found themselves with an annual commitment to undertake and evidence CPD in order to continue in work. The revocation of the 2007 regulations in 2012 has meant that the pendulum is currently on its way back; CPD is no longer mandatory, but something that teachers and employers are strongly encouraged to undertake and facilitate.

There are advantages to this situation. There is little doubt that the compulsory element of CPD under the 2007 regulations encouraged a bureaucracy surrounding the collection of evidence and a 'tick-box' approach whereby CPD was undertaken primarily to maintain the licence to practise rather than for any intrinsic motivation. This raised concern that mandatory professional development had the paradoxical effect of de-professionalising the sector in that ownership of CPD was managed by a national political agency. On the other hand, there is also no doubt that the work done by the IfL has provided those working within FE with a considerable body of resources and advice that can be invaluable for you when you plan your own professional development; there is plenty of guidance and support available.

The IfL's approach to professional development is based on the concept of the reflective practitioner, which you will doubtless remember from Chapter 5. Hitching describes the process thus.

> *You as practitioner are central to the process (of reflective practice)... it is integral to the whole process of professional growth. It begins with... examining your practice as a means to identifying your professional needs. It continues with you setting out these needs clearly as a set of measurable objectives and engaging in activities to achieve them.*

(Hitching, 2008, p 13)

The attraction of this approach is that it can be applied whatever your stage of professional development. It is likely that at the start of your career – what Gregorc called the 'beginning' stage – there will be emphasis on the theoretical understanding of good teaching practice that forms the basis of most initial teacher training courses. As you gain experience and work towards Gregorc's 'fully functioning' stage, the professional knowledge that you gain from this experience will constitute an increasing element of your reflective practice, creating the opportunity to integrate both theory and your experience in your professional practice.

Identifying your professional development needs

No matter what stage you have reached in your professional career, the starting point for managing your professional development is to identify your professional development needs. How the reflective model for doing this works in practice can be illustrated by the story of Sean.

CASE STUDY

Sean

Sean is 45 years old and has held a full-time post at a large FE college for just over a year. He is an experienced teacher who has six years' experience as an instructor in electronics in the army. He holds a C&G 7407 teaching certificate and is keen to make a permanent career in FE.

His first year in FE has been challenging but enjoyable, teaching full-time and part-time electronics courses. This year, however, Sean has encountered problems. The main one concerns a class in numeracy to learners on a return-to-work course that he has been asked to teach. Most of the learners basically do not want to be there and attend reluctantly in order to retain their benefits. In spite of spending hours planning lessons and trying to make the subject interesting, Sean has not managed to gain a rapport with these learners who have become increasingly fractious and unwilling to work. He is beginning to feel out of his depth as this is his first experience of teaching an ill-motivated group of learners who do not do what they are told. Teaching with the backup of army discipline is starting to seem like a luxury and he is beginning to dread 9.00–12.00 every Tuesday and Thursday morning.

Sean's second problem is that he is getting behind with the coursework on the B Eng degree that he is studying with the Open University (OU). He started this course soon after he was appointed, with the encouragement of the college management who are always keen to support their staff in improving their specialist subject qualifications. There never seems to be any time for studying at the end of an exhausting day of meetings, assessments, administration and teaching. When he returns home each night there is usually a pile of marking or preparation to do, and he is conscious that the job is beginning to affect the quality of his family life. All in all he is beginning to feel the strain of a very demanding professional job and decides he needs to talk to Kumar, the experienced teacher who had been nominated to support Sean during the first two years of his appointment.

Critical thinking activity

»   *How would you describe Sean's professional development needs as shown by this story?*

»   *Which need should take priority, and why?*

There are several issues that emerge from this story. Firstly, Sean's OU course will benefit his career prospects but there is a price to pay. OU degrees are intellectually demanding and require significant personal commitment in terms of time. At this stage of his professional development, while he is coming to terms with a new job in an unfamiliar organisation, he may have to reconsider the priority he gives to this venture.

Added to this, Sean is clearly worried about the demands of his job on his work/life balance. Being professional does not mean giving your whole life to the job, and creating an appropriate balance between work and the rest of your life is important for your health and well-being. This is definitely your responsibility and you need strategies to check that you are not becoming an obsessive workaholic.

The numeracy class is another significant issue for Sean's professional development. Although he has significant teaching experience, Sean has not been faced by a challenging and unmotivated group of learners before. He may theoretically know the strategies to employ in this situation, but it is another thing entirely to put them into practice. There is a clear development need here, and it has to be addressed. Until he faces the problem it is likely to become more critical, adding to his stress and reinforcing the learners' pre-conceived ideas about the irrelevance of their course.

In summary, Sean has at least three identifiable development needs: to improve his ability to manage difficult classes, to manage his specialist subject studies more effectively and to find strategies for maintaining a healthy work/life balance. He needs to have a logical method of identifying and prioritising his needs, and this could be centred around appraisal. You may already be working for an organisation that has an established appraisal system that is linked to staff development needs, and such schemes nearly always have an element of self-appraisal as part of the appraisal process. It is this element that should form the starting point for identifying your development needs, and the good news is that you do not need to belong to a formal appraisal scheme to do this. Anyone can take advantage of the process, and in Sean's case it would be a good tactic to pursue in preparation for his conversation with Kumar.

Self-appraisal

Self-appraisal involves reflection on what has happened professionally during a previous period, normally annual, as a basis for looking forward to the future. Typically it includes the following key questions.

•   What has gone well over the period?

•   What things have not gone so well?

- Why have they not gone so well?

- What needs to happen to improve these areas of difficulty?

- What support do you need?

- What changes in the way you work do you want to happen in the future?

Responses to these questions need to be set in the context not only of your own aspirations, but they need to take into account your work environment, the needs of your organisation and what realistic level of support would be possible. Naturally, if you can tailor your needs to fit the development priorities of your organisation, the better your chance of being successful in obtaining support. Support for Sean's OU course is more likely to be forthcoming if the college needs an electronics graduate to teach a particular course, less likely if it is seen as irrelevant to the college's development plans and merely fulfilling a personal aspiration.

It might also be helpful to design a self-evaluation prompt list when you prepare answers to the key questions. Here is a suggested prompt list that should ensure you cover most of the relevant issues.

- What are the key tasks and responsibilities of your present post?

- What are the main implications of your employer's development plans for your work?

- What parts of your job give you most satisfaction?

- How can you build on the satisfying parts of your job?

- What skills do you have that could be used to greater advantage?

- What aspects of your job have not gone as well as you hoped?

- How could you improve these areas of performance?

- What skills or areas of expertise would you like to develop?

You may have noted that much of this is concerned with relatively short-term issues, a reaction to concerns that Sean has about his current work situation. It will also be useful for him to find a quiet period when he can reflect on his long-term development needs, and these depend on his long-term career aspirations. What does he want to be doing professionally in five or ten years' time? Does he want to develop within his present role or work towards a change of responsibilities? What skills, experience and qualifications will he need in order to have a chance of succeeding? If this can be written down and tabulated, it provides a base document for professional development that can be reviewed periodically and amended in the light of your experience during the review period. This is all about a continuous process of professional development, a process that evolves and brings new insights to your professionalism as you progress through your career.

Critical thinking activity: identifying development needs

» *Identify and prioritise your own immediate and long-term professional development needs. What criteria did you use to make your judgements?*

Planning your professional development

Sean's story also touches on the outcomes of the analysis of his professional development. Once a need is identified, how is it going to be met? His story continues.

CASE STUDY

Sean and Kumar

Kumar was not surprised when Sean told him about problems with the numeracy class. He had already received feedback from other teachers who found the class difficult and was aware that managing and motivating a group like this was outside Sean's previous teaching experience. He also realised that the problem could not be ignored or shelved. As a professional, Sean needed to possess the skills to motivate reluctant learners. Both employers and college management have the right to expect high standards of teaching and this would certainly include being able to teach uncommitted or resentful learners.

Kumar also saw that Sean was stressed and having difficulty in coping with his workload. However, he felt that if Sean could be given support to manage the numeracy class more effectively this would relieve the stress and reverse the vicious circle whereby the more worried he became about teaching this group the more his stress increased. Consequently, improving Sean's skill in motivating uncommitted learners and dealing with disruptive classroom behaviour was priority number one.

Critical thinking activity

» *What advice and support could Kumar offer in order to improve Sean's ability to deal more effectively with this class?*

In Sean's case there are several approaches that he could consider to improve his classroom management skills and be more effective in dealing with the problems of his numeracy class. Traditionally, the typical response to someone who had an identified training need was to send them on a course. This is an approach with severe limitations. It is probably effective in very specific circumstances, such as learning how to operate a new piece of computer software or to introduce a change in examination procedures, but even here there are significant restrictions. The organisation loses a member of staff for the duration of the course, often incurs substantial expense to send someone away for training and has little control over the quality and relevance of the input.

In-house courses avoid some of these disadvantages, and are often used effectively to meet a development need that affects a number of staff, such as updating on first-aid training or the introduction of a new enrolment form. Such courses are often incorporated into staff training days. It is unlikely, however, that such training will be available or appropriate to solve Sean's problems with his numeracy class. What is needed here is the opportunity for him to try things out, to put new ideas into practice, together with support from a fellow professional who has a high level of skill in motivating challenging learners.

There are several professional development activities that may be effective. The first is the use of a mentor, a critical friend who is experienced at managing difficult groups and who can give constructive advice and offer some ideas on how to manage this class. This can be supplemented by giving Sean the opportunity to watch his mentor in action, and also by allowing the mentor to observe Sean's teaching. The advantage of these approaches is that they are specifically focused on Sean's problems and they give practical support based on proven professional expertise in classroom management.

In summary, there is a range of activities that can be considered for Sean to improve his ability to deal with difficult learners. Mentoring, observation of an experienced teacher, peer observation and research into classroom management techniques are all activities that, taken separately or in combination, could be used effectively.

There is a general point that can be made about planning professional development activities. You should be able to define what outcome you want to attain from undertaking the activity. This is often referred to in the context of 'SMART' targets; that is, outcomes that are:

* **S**pecific   What do you want to accomplish?

* **M**easurable   How will you know when it is accomplished?

* **A**ttainable   How can it be accomplished?

* **R**elevant   Is it worthwhile?

* **T**ime bound   When will it be completed?

Not all professional development activities fit neatly into this approach which is often used by management in the administration of appraisal schemes. Nevertheless it is a useful set of criteria to apply when planning your own professional development.

Critical thinking activity: planning professional development

» Select one of the development needs you identified in the previous activity (preferably a high-priority need) and research the most appropriate ways in which this need might be met. You may find Hitching's book (2008), details of which are listed at the end of this chapter, a useful starting point.

» What are the advantages and limitations of the development activities you have chosen? Use both educational theory and your own experience in considering this issue.

Undertaking your professional development activities

Once you have embarked on some form of professional development activity, much of the benefit can be wasted if you do not monitor what you are doing. This point is well illustrated by the continuing story of Sean.

CASE STUDY

Sean's observation

As a result of his conversation with Kumar, Sean has just observed Paula, an experienced teacher in Communication Studies, teaching interview techniques to his difficult numeracy group.

Paula has been very helpful and supportive. A day before the class, she talked through with Sean what she was trying to do, described how she dealt with the most apathetic and challenging members of the group, and gave him a copy of her lesson plan with notes on individual learners. Before the class started Paula set out the room for a small group role-play she had planned and explained to Sean why she had allocated particular roles to certain learners. Sean waited with some apprehension for the class to begin.

Two hours later, Sean felt exhausted and depressed. Paula had taught the group at a whirlwind pace. She was an inspiring teacher: her enthusiasm was infectious, she seemed to like all the learners and they responded positively because she clearly wanted them to succeed. Even Gavin, who spent his time in Sean's classes saying he was bored and distracting anyone who wanted to work, showed some enthusiasm and completed the tasks. In short, Sean was overwhelmed and feared he would never be able to teach like Paula.

Paula had to leave immediately after the lesson, but arranged to meet Sean after work to discuss her lesson and give him the opportunity to ask any questions.

Critical thinking activity

» *What do you think Sean learned from this activity that might help him to teach the numeracy group more effectively?*

» *What specific issues should he raise with Paula?*

It is not clear from the narrative how much preparation Sean had done for this observation. If he just went into the class with a general idea to watch what was going on it is probably not surprising that he felt depressed at the end: he had just watched a professional demonstrating teaching skills of a high order that confirmed his own feelings of inadequacy.

On the other hand, it is also possible that Sean would have discussed in advance with Paula the rationale behind the purpose and structure of her lesson plan and how she was going to manage the class. In particular he would have been interested in how she planned to deal with learners like Gavin and tackle the lack of motivation and potential disruption in the group. During the lesson he may have noted specific things that Paula did which he could use in his lessons and taken notes on how she dealt with individual learners who routinely gave him a lot of grief. All this should give him plenty of material to discuss with Paula when he met her after the class as a prelude to identifying things he could do that would make his future classes more effective.

Critical reflection and CPD

Critical reflection is an important feature of CPD. If critical reflection is a key professional attitude in your teaching, as argued in Chapter 5, it is no less fundamental as a driving force in your own development. The cyclical nature of reflective practice, the feature of learning from a wide variety of theoretical and practical experiences, together with the discipline of recording your reflections are all professional attributes that determine the quality of your CPD. Its value can be illustrated by the way Sean reflected on his observation of Paula.

CASE STUDY

Sean's reflection

Here is an extract from Sean's reflective journal following his observation of Paula's lesson.

I've just witnessed a great lesson – it was so good that I don't think I'll ever be able to teach as well as Paula does, so I ended up feeling pretty inadequate. Most of the time was taken up by an interview role-play where the class was divided into four groups of five – two interviewers, one interviewee and two observers in each group. The whole class had been briefed in the previous session and they then spent the first 20 minutes of this session with the interviewers preparing the questions to ask, the interviewees trying to second guess the questions and the observers discussing what they would look for. Paula constantly went round each group but didn't interfere as long as they were working OK. Then they were allowed half an hour to do the interviews, and Paula asked me to monitor what was going on in two of the groups, but only intervene if they weren't working or someone was being disruptive. This overran a bit, but there was still time for them to fill in the evaluation forms that Paula had prepared and then finish with ten minutes for whole-class discussion.

I've been trying to work out why this lesson worked so well and why all the learners were willing to get involved rather than mess about like they do with me. In no particular order this is what I think.

Lots of learner activity: They never seemed to have a moment to mess about, and when they looked likely to be distracted Paula was there to bring them back on course.

Lots of encouragement: I noticed that Paula frequently praised the way individuals tried to answer questions and contributed to the group work. Like when she publicly complimented Sam, who never seems to do anything in my classes, on how she had written a couple of questions to ask: Sam's face positively lit up when she heard this.

Lots of preparation: Not only the handouts and briefing sheets, which were great (it must have taken her hours to do!), but also setting the room out beforehand, complete with name tags, pens, paper, etc. And all the learners knew exactly what their role was because Paula had negotiated this with them during the previous class. Note negotiated, not allocated, so they felt some sort of ownership of what they were doing.

Consistency: Paula told me that when she first started teaching this class she had a half hour where she negotiated the ground rules for her sessions – agreeing what she would do and what she expected in return. Interestingly, she asked the class what rules they would like, and adopted most of them. She has had a few problems since then, but by and large the learners have stuck to their side of the bargain. It seems to work, because when Linda started to disrupt her group by talking loudly about her boyfriend it was the group that told her to save it till later; Paula didn't have to intervene at all.

Relevance: Paula negotiated with the group what topics they would cover, asking for their suggestions to add to her own list. And each class member had chosen the jobs they would apply for from adverts in the local paper. Rajesh had even been invited for an interview and used the session to have a dummy run.

Knowing each individual learner: Paula had spent a lot of time at the start of the course talking to each learner and finding out as much as possible about them. She'd even been to the Job Centre on behalf of Jodie who has a lot of problems with literacy and is afraid to talk to people about it. I had a word with one of the groups I was monitoring and they all said that they felt Paula was on their side, wanted them to succeed and cared about them.

So what can I do to be more like Paula? I'm thinking of trying to start again with this group, to tell them that I think we've got off on the wrong foot and have a session like Paula had to establish ground rules and negotiate the things we can do in class. I also need to have a chat with each one of them to get to know them better – a sort of get-to-know-you tutorial. And I've got some ideas as to how to make numeracy more relevant to them. For instance, most of them do the lottery and I could get them to work out the odds of winning on each type of lottery ticket. And Jason has just bought a motorbike on hire purchase, so there is scope for some numeracy there as well. Perhaps I could make a list of suggestions for them to consider when I have this negotiating session. I'd also like to ask Paula if she could come and watch me teach the group in the next week or so, but not until I've tried out some of these ideas.

Critical thinking activity

» Does this journal entry meet the criteria for critical reflection detailed in Chapter 5? Is it analytical, reflective, critical?

» To what extent does it illustrate the professional quality of a teacher who sees her/ himself as a self-critical, collaborative and creative learner?

The first paragraph of the journal is essentially descriptive and clearly not reflective, apart from a general statement about feeling inadequate. The second paragraph, however, contains a fairly detailed and objective analysis of Paula's teaching technique that Sean has identified as potentially relevant to solving his own class management problems, and he then reflects on how he could use some of these tactics in future.

CPD and dual professionalism

One of the defining features of professionalism in FE is that of its dual nature, in the sense that you are a professional twice over, acting as a professional teacher and a professional in your subject specialism. This feature has implications for your professional development. In addition to developing your teaching skills you also need to keep up to date in your subject area and retain your credibility with your learners and colleagues. This raises some difficult issues, particularly in those subject areas like ICT where the rate of change is rapid. Sean considered this problem when he reflected on ways to keep up to date as an engineer.

CASE STUDY

Sean: engineer or teacher?

Here is an extract from Sean's reflective journal.

I feel I'm getting out of touch. It came home to me today when I was teaching the level 3 electronics class. They're a good group, attending one day a week on part-time day release, and most of them work at KV Electronics, a medium-sized firm in the town. A couple of the lads were talking to me about how KV is investing in surface micromachining and I had to admit I knew little about it and I feel that unless I do something about keeping more up to date I'll lose credibility with groups like this.

I reckon I'm doing what I can. There's the OU course and I'm a member of the Institution of Engineering and Technology (IET), but when it comes down to it I've not been working in a real electronics workshop for three years and it's beginning to show. When I was in the army it wasn't so bad because although I was an instructor, a lot of the work was on the job and I was always in the workshops. My classes knew I could do the practical stuff because they saw me being involved all the time. Now I'm in danger of them seeing me as one of the 'if you can't do, teach' brigade.

The trouble is there's so much else to do in college; all the admin, marking, meetings, teaching and learning how to cope with bolshie numeracy students! I must talk about this to Kumar.

Critical thinking activity

» *What would you advise Sean to do in order to keep up to date in his subject specialism?*

» *What priority should be given to this aspect of his professional development?*

Theoretically there are plenty of options for Sean to keep in touch with developments in electronics. These include visits to factories like KV, attending electronics conferences, going to local IET meetings or even arranging a short secondment to an electronics firm. In practical terms, however, this has to be measured against his other development needs, and the time and resource constraints that apply in such a busy job. The priority given to any of these activities goes back to Sean's self-appraisal of what is most important and urgent for him to focus on.

Evaluating your professional development

How successful has your professional development been over the past year? How do you know? What could have been done better? Answers to these and similar questions are critical in evaluating the effectiveness of all the activities you have undertaken to enhance your professionalism and help your learners to the best of your ability. This evaluative process involves a systematic approach to gathering a wide range of opinions and data to support your own feelings and conclusions.

If you are involved in a formal appraisal system, this will doubtless include a process for evaluating the effectiveness of professional development activities undertaken as part of the scheme. At a minimum, the annual appraisal meeting will review and record how well such activities have been accomplished, and the more information to support your conclusions the better. In the case of Sean and his numeracy class this would probably include both quantitative and qualitative evidence.

Quantitative data:

- test results;
- retention rate;
- attendance records, etc.

Qualitative data:

- reports on peer observations (such as those we've discussed regarding Paula and Kumar, for example) and observations as part of the institution's quality assurance system;
- learner feedback, such as formative and summative evaluation sheets and informal comment;
- employer/sponsor feedback;
- your lesson evaluations and professional development journal entries.

This is not an exhaustive list, but gives an idea of the type of information that can be used to back up your own feelings about the success or otherwise of the things you have done to improve your professional skills and knowledge, and to give an indication of what you need to do next.

If you are not involved in an appraisal system, the need for a systematic approach to evaluating your professional development is, if anything, even more important. One difference is that you can design this system yourself, which at least has the advantage that you can tailor the scheme to your own specific needs. Another difference is that you may well have to take responsibility for involving others in your plans – colleagues, your mentor, your line manager, your learners and so on. In any event, the knowledge of how you are going to assess the success of your development activities objectively and comprehensively before you start undertaking them is a good sign of your professional approach to your work.

Critical thinking activity: evaluating professional development

» *How do you evaluate your own professional development? Research the theory and practice of personal development appraisal schemes and incorporate any relevant processes into the evaluation of your own CPD.*

Conclusion

Professional teachers are always learning, and enthusiasm for their specialism and for constant improvement in their teaching skills are key features of professional practice. It is not easy. Pressure of work in contemporary FE and attempts by recent governments to introduce professionalism by mandate have had the effect of dampening enthusiasm in much of the sector. This is a pity because imposed professionalism runs counter to the key feature of a professional's love of learning for its own sake. However, one legacy of the 2007 regulations is that they facilitated the design and provision of a wealth of advice and resources that you can use to develop your professional practice.

Chapter reflections

» *A truly professional teacher is one who is a perennial learner, constantly self-critical, creative and enthusiastic about their specialism and their teaching.*

» *Your professional development needs and activities are cyclical and develop throughout the different stages of your career.*

» *Systematic identification of your development needs, together with logical planning and evaluation of your development activities are key features of your professional development.*

» *Critical reflection and self-evaluation are essential skills in evaluating professional development activities.*

Taking it further

Avis, J, Fisher, R and Thompson, P (2010) *Teaching in Lifelong Learning: A Guide to Theory and Practice.* Maidenhead: McGraw Hill Education.
This contains a detailed section (Chapter 22) on career planning and CPD.

Hitching, J (2008) *Maintaining Your Licence to Practise.* Exeter: Learning Matters.
This is a comprehensive guide to CPD as envisaged by the IfL.

References

Dreyfus, S and Dreyfus, H (1980) *A Five-Stage Model of the Mental Activities Involved in Directed Skill Acquisition.* Washington, DC: Storming Media.

Eraut, M (1994) *Developing Professional Knowledge and Competence.* Abingdon: Routledge Falmer.

Hitching, J (2008) *Maintaining Your Licence to Practise.* Exeter: Learning Matters.

LLUK (2007) *New Overarching Professional Standards for Teachers, Tutors and Trainers in the Lifelong Learning Sector,* London: LLUK.

Wallace, S (2007) *Teaching, Tutoring and Training in the Lifelong Learning Sector.* Exeter: Learning Matters.

9 Conclusion: taking pride

On Armistice Day, 11 November 1918, Captain Fred Roberts and Lieutenant Jack Pearson of the 12th Battalion, Sherwood Foresters regiment, stand in a command post on the Somme and toast the end of the fighting and take pride in a job well done. In their case, it was a surprising and outstanding accomplishment. It was surprising because, in addition to fighting the enemy, they had produced throughout the war over 20 publications of a witty and sophisticated satirical newspaper much like the modern *Private Eye*, aimed at resolutely cheering up the troops on the Front. The newspaper, *The Wipers Times*, contained wry jokes, witty articles, poems and tongue-in-cheek 'adverts' referring to the awful circumstances of the war they found themselves in, the dangerous conditions they faced daily.

It was an outstanding accomplishment because Roberts and Pearson needed to overcome numerous frustrations and irritations. First there was the bureaucracy: the scheme was frowned upon by enraged staff officers who thought that war was not to be trivialised and did their best to shut down the publication. Then there was the lack of resources: printing machinery, ink, paper and so on were in short supply at the Front. Finally, there were the time constraints, interferences and distractions: this was trench warfare and it isn't hard to imagine the difficulties of producing a newspaper in the trenches, surrounded by mud, rats, shelling, gas and death.

At first glance, this story doesn't fit in with the features of professionalism described in this book. After all, Roberts and Pearson hadn't been trained in journalism, they were not being paid for their work and they did not belong to a professional body; by these criteria, they were amateurs. However, their story vividly illustrates two key features of the professionalism of individuals; the constant striving for excellence and the need to continue to learn and develop their skills for as long as they were involved in producing the newspaper. All this was achieved in a hostile environment (literally!) over a long period of time with little support from the hierarchy. You might recognise echoes of this situation in your role as a teacher in contemporary FE. Their rewards were almost entirely those of self-fulfilment, from the satisfaction of a job well done and the knowledge that they had done something to improve the lives of others. For Roberts and Pearson this meant the soldiers at the Front; for you it means your learners.

This book has made a distinction between corporate and individual professionalism and the focus has been on the latter. However, in your role as a professional teacher in FE there is no way of avoiding the impact of corporate professionalism on the sector, with interventionist government policies dominating the FE landscape for over 20 years. You will certainly not need to be reminded that the sector has been subject to an ever increasing amount of government regulation that has significantly affected the lives of all teachers in the sector. The incorporation of colleges in 1992, followed by increasing government regulation since 2001, illustrates a strategy based on the belief that a successful economy and prosperous society is dependent on a skilled workforce that is trained and constantly updated through a world-class vocational education system.

The effect of all this on FE teachers has been drastic. Elliott, interviewing teachers post-1992, concluded that

> the speed and scope of change is unprecedented. Lecturers have experienced acute loss of control of their work situation... There is a real tension in colleges between the management imposed imperatives of satisfying quantitative performance indicators and lecturers' conceptions and priorities based on their value judgements.
>
> (Elliott, 1996, p 60)

This conclusion was supported by research conducted by the lecturers' union, the UCU, in 2008:

> While staff are proud to work in the FE sector, many feel negative about the particular institutions in which they work. Only around a third of lecturers would recommend their organisation as a good place to work. Large numbers of experienced staff are planning or hoping to leave their college. Many confirm the unhappiness and frustration that UCU knows is widespread in colleges... More than half of teaching staff say their workspace and equipment are inadequate, even higher proportions of part-time staff report this. And 50% of teaching staff feel their job is insecure.
>
> The most worrying findings of the research reveal a workforce under considerable strain. In common with other professionals in the UK, many people in further education feel that they are under stress and struggling to achieve the right balance between their work and home lives.
>
> (Villeneuve-Smith, 2008, p 1)

Thus the FE sector post-incorporation has not always been a happy place to work. Teachers have found themselves with increased teaching hours, worsening conditions of service, a heavy administrative burden and a perceived diminution of their autonomy. There is also evidence that morale in the sector was adversely affected following the introduction of the 2007 regulations. The Lingfield report noted a

> degree of fearfulness expressed by many lecturers... (who saw the 2007 regulations) as offering some symbolic protection against arbitrary changes to worsen their

circumstances carried out by employers, or by government and its agencies...
Professional teaching staff, in a sector always acknowledged to be central in
achieving national economic success... too often say they feel so vulnerable as
to need protection by a statutory instrument they know to be otiose. There is a
confidence deficit in the professionalism of the further education sector.

(BIS, October 2012, p 13)

This policy of creating a professional FE workforce through central government regulation was significantly modified following the publication of the Lingfield report in 2012. The change of government in 2010, combined with a boycott by FE teachers of IfL registration in 2011, led to a fundamental rethink of the policy, with the shortcomings of the mandatory approach to professionalism succinctly described in the interim Lingfield report:

Most of the national effort has been made in the wrong place: towards standards,
regulations and compulsion, rather than towards fostering a deep and shared
commitment to real 'bottom up' professionalism among FE employers and staff.

(BIS, March 2012, p 14)

So what was the solution? According to Lingfield, it was to return more power to the profession.

Organisations in further education should be left alone, in near autonomy, to get
on with serving their students, their local communities and the employers on whom
national economic renewal depends. Our conclusions, then, are intended to help
create an environment in which the professionalism of further education lecturers,
instructors, workplace supervisors and assessors might naturally flourish, without
interference... Further Education in this country is a developing and dynamic entity,
naturally and properly diverse; we believe that its future success depends upon
placing trust in the professionals who work within it to direct it, take its decisions
and promulgate its priorities.

(BIS, October 2012, p 4)

As this approach had much political support, the regulatory pendulum is now starting to swing the other way: less central control, more local autonomy. An inevitable consequence of this is an increase in variation of approach to professionalism as stakeholders negotiate in accordance with their local priorities. You may be fortunate enough to work in an environment where your individual professionalism is encouraged and funded: support for gaining qualifications, planned CPD, effective mentoring and so forth. But the tensions between corporate and individual professional needs are a permanent feature of any occupational environment and you may not be lucky enough to find such a supportive employer. This brings us back to the question of how you can develop your own professionalism in a world that may be unsympathetic or even obstructive.

It has been the intention of this book to provide answers to this question. One of the characteristics of professionalism is to recognise the potential conflict between the needs of your institution and your own professional needs and to reconcile the conflict as best you can. This is a dilemma well summarised by Julian Baggini.

The most demanding feature of professionalism in general [is perhaps] the ability to deliver on the corporate entity's desired goals, whether or not these are your goals or even that you fully approve of them. It is not professional to reject the demands placed on you and do your own thing.

But... the true professional never abandons his or her own judgment or values entirely. Professionalism is marked by an ability to deliver in ways which are as commensurate as possible with your own vision... and what your values are.

(Baggini, 2005, pp 10–11)

Professionalism at its best is encapsulated in the final paragraph of this quotation. Gleeson and Shain (1999) give several examples of how FE managers and teachers have squared the circle of retaining their own judgement and values in the face of managerial demands. They noted

a form of artful pragmatism that reconciles professional and managerial interests... they accept some aspects of the new FE work culture... but also retain their professional values and bend with change. [They]... adopt an approach of strategic compliance... maintaining a commitment to educational and professional values in support of students and collegiality.

(Gleeson and Shain, 1999, pp 482, 488)

This sceptical and pragmatic approach is, however, only a start. The key to success lies in your interpretation of the word 'professionalism'. Although you can argue for ever about the precise meaning of the word, some things stand out as important common features. It is these features that define the essence of professionalism.

- Know yourself, your values, beliefs and emotions and how they determine your professional identity.

- Use your professional curiosity to understand the diversity of your learners and establish an inclusive and effective professional relationship with them.

- Develop your faculty for critical reflection as a key professional ability that guides and develops your teaching skills throughout your teaching career.

- Identify, develop and value your own individual brand of teaching and enjoy the interaction with your learners.

- Be sensitive to the nature of your institution as a learning organisation and develop your communication, empathy, time management, organisational and administrative skills in dealing with people you work with.

- Be a perennial learner, constantly self-critical, creative and enthusiastic about your specialism and your teaching.

If you can do these things, they can form the bedrock of professionalism in one of the most rewarding occupations in the world. In spite of all the frustrations, you can, like the men who produced 'The Wipers Times' for the troops at the Front in 1918, congratulate yourself on a job well done. And you can take pride in helping learners achieve their goals and changing people's lives for the better.

References

Baggini, J (2005) What Professionalism Means for Teachers Today, in *Education Review*, 18(2) (Summer). London: NUT.

BIS (March 2012) *Professionalism in Further Education – Interim Report*. London: BIS.

BIS (October 2012) *Professionalism in Further Education – Final Report*. London: BIS.

Elliott, G (1996) *Crisis and Change in Vocational Education and Training*. London: Jessica Kingsley.

Gleeson, D and Shain, F (1999) Managing Ambiguity: Between Markets and Managerialism – A Case Study of Middle Managers in Further Education, *Sociological Review*, 47(3).

Villeneuve-Smith, F, Munoz, S and McKenzie, E (2008) *FE Colleges: The Frontline under Pressure?* London: Learning and Skills Network.

Appendix A: LLUK Professional Standards

Domain A, Professional values and practice (Extract)

The practice of teaching is underpinned by a set of professional values that should be observed by all teachers, tutors and trainers in all settings. This domain sets the standards for these values and their associated commitments.

Professional values

Teachers in the lifelong learning sector value:

AS 1 All learners, their progress and development, their learning goals and aspirations and the experience they bring to their learning.

AS 2 Learning, its potential to benefit people emotionally, intellectually, socially and economically, and its contribution to community sustainability.

AS 3 Equality, diversity and inclusion in relation to learners, the workforce and the community.

AS 4 Reflection and evaluation of their own practice and their continuing professional development as teachers.

AS 5 Collaboration with other individuals, groups and/or organisations with a legitimate interest in the progress and development of learners.

They are committed to:

AS 6 The application of agreed codes of practice and the maintenance of a safe environment.

AS 7 Improving the quality of their practice.

Professional knowledge and understanding

Teachers in the lifelong learning sector know and understand:

AK 1.1 What motivates learners to learn and the importance of learners' experience and aspirations.

AK 2.1 Ways in which learning has the potential to change lives.

AK 2.2 Ways in which learning promotes the emotional, intellectual, social and economic well-being of individuals and the population as a whole.

AK 3.1 Issues of equality, diversity and inclusion.

AK 4.1 Principles, frameworks and theories which underpin good practice in learning and teaching.

AK 4.2 The impact of own practice on individuals and their learning.

AK 4.3 Ways to reflect, evaluate and use research to develop own practice, and to share good practice with others.

AK 5.1 Ways to communicate and collaborate with colleagues and/or others to enhance learners' experience.

AK 5.2 The need for confidentiality, respect and trust in communicating with others about learners.

AK 6.1 Relevant statutory requirements and codes of practice.

AK 6.2 Ways to apply relevant statutory requirements and the underpinning principles.

AK 7.1 Organisational systems and processes for recording learner information.

AK 7.2 Own role in the quality cycle.

AK 7.3 Ways to implement improvements based on feedback received.

Appendix B: The Institute for Learning

Code of Professional Practice (Extract)

The Institute for Learning's Code of Professional Practice came into force on 1 April 2008. The Code was developed by the profession for the profession and it outlines the behaviours expected of members – for the benefit of learners, employers, the profession and the wider community.

- Integrity
- Respect
- Care
- Practice
- Disclosure
- Responsibility.

Behaviour 1: Professional integrity

The members shall:

1. Meet their professional responsibilities consistent with the Institute's professional values.

2. Use reasonable professional judgement when discharging differing responsibilities and obligations to learners, colleagues, institution and the wider profession.

3. Uphold the reputation of the profession by never unjustly or knowingly damaging the professional reputation of another or furthering their own position unfairly at the expense of another.

4. Comply with all reasonable assessment and quality procedures and obligations.

5. Uphold the standing and reputation of the Institute and not knowingly undermine or misrepresent its views nor their Institute membership, any qualification or professional status.

Behaviour 2: Respect

The members shall at all times:

1.   Respect the rights of learners and colleagues in accordance with relevant legislation and organisation requirements.

2.   Act in a manner which recognises diversity as an asset and does not discriminate in respect of race, gender, disability and/or learning difficulty, age, sexual orientation or religion and belief.

Behaviour 3: Reasonable care

The members shall take reasonable care to ensure the safety and welfare of learners and comply with relevant statutory provisions to support their well-being and development.

Behaviour 4: Professional practice

The members shall provide evidence to the Institute that they have complied with the current Institute CPD policy and guidelines.

Behaviour 5: Criminal offence disclosure

Any member shall notify the Institute as soon as practicable after cautioning or conviction for a criminal offence. The Institute reserves the right to act on such information through its disciplinary process.

Behaviour 6: Responsibility during Institute investigations

A member shall use their best endeavours to assist in any investigation and shall not seek to dissuade, penalise or discourage a person from bringing a complaint against any member, interfere with or otherwise compromise due process.

Behaviour 7: Responsibility to the Institute

The members shall at all times act in accordance with the Institute's conditions of membership which will be subject to change from time to time.

Index